Concepts in the Social Sciences

Postmodernity

Second Edition

David Lyon

Open University Press
Buckingham

Open University Press
Celtic Court
22 Ballmoor
Buckingham
MK18 1XW

email: enquiries@openup.co.uk
world wide web: http://www.openup.co.uk

First Published 1999

A catalogue record of this book is available from the British Library

ISBN 0 335 20144 X (pbk)   0 335 20145 8 (hbk)

Typeset by Type Study, Scarborough
Printed in Great Britain by St Edmundsbury Press, Bury St Edmunds,
Suffolk

In memory of my father
Harold Fullarton Lyon 1921–1990

He founded Strathcarron Hospice, Central Scotland;
tempering modern medicine with compassion

Contents

Preface to the First Edition

Yesterday evening my children and I came across a photo of me as a toddler, wearing my father's shoes. As I write, I feel a bit like I must have felt then, struggling along in something too big for me. This book attempts the impossible: a brief account of postmodernity. Impossible because postmodernity has many possible meanings, and thus brevity will not do it justice. Much is left out. Let me comment on each factor.

Postmodernity is a multi-layered concept that alerts us to a variety of major social and cultural changes taking place at the end of the twentieth century within many 'advanced' societies. Rapid technological change, involving telecommunications and computer power, shifting political concerns, the rise of social movements, especially those with a gender, green, ethnic and racial focus, are all implicated. But the question is even bigger: is modernity itself, as a social-cultural entity, disintegrating, including the whole grand edifice of Enlightenment world-views? And, is a new type of society appearing, perhaps structured around consumers and consumption rather than workers and production?

Grounds for including and excluding material on the debate over postmodernity arise from two considerations. One is the desire to make a readable introduction to what is now a very complex field of study. I hope that, though I have not discussed all aspects or authors in detail, the reader will be able to fill out the picture from further references in the notes. The other is my own background of research and writing: I am concerned with theories of social change, especially as they relate to secularization and to the social dimensions of information and communication technologies.

Acknowledgements

I am deeply indebted to friends, colleagues, students and members of my family for their help and encouragement in writing this book. Those whose comments have obliged me to rethink several issues include Marya Bootsma, Annette Burfoot, Ken Jacobson, Richard Middleton, Ray Morrow, Philip Sampson, Barry Smart, Bin-ky Tan, Ivan Varga and Gianni Vattimo. I am responsible for the end product. Queen's University supported some of the work with a grant from the Advisory Research Committee. The best assistance from Sue, Tim, Abi, Josh and Min came in the form of enjoyable diversion. Postmodernity, dad? Get real.

David Lyon, 1994

Preface to the
Second Edition

Reality refuses to go away, even when the air is thickly postmodern. I curled in front of a log fire by candlelight to work on this preface, but not by romantic choice. A freak ice storm had brought down trees and power lines in eastern Ontario and Quebec, wreaking havoc with modern conveniences. No power, no phone, no Internet. No radio or TV either, for the local stations, cable systems and relays were also down, although paradoxically, our situation was already a media event elsewhere. That was a postmodern twist. Others knew better than we did what was happening all around us.

Apart from that, we saw little local evidence of postmodernity right then in Kingston. Temporarily, we had a lot of difficulty being modern, as transport and communications shut down and a state of emergency was declared. Emergency? Well, we were unprepared for the problem of how to keep warm in a Canadian winter without the taken-for-granted electricity supply which also affects water purification and other essential services. Even today, two weeks after the storm, some shiver and make do with no power supply. But they are mainly far from the centres to which help first came, for, in a curious irony, it was the relatively well-off urbanites who were first and worst hit by the storm.

Well, perhaps that's a shift from modern times, too, when the most vulnerable were the poor, the displaced, the marginal? No, all were hit by that weird weather. But it may mean that the disturbances, the discontents and the disillusionment of today have distinctive postmodern features. We shall see. At the very least, an ice storm leaves lessons in its wake, that there are no guarantees, no certainties in the world of technoscience and cyberspace. Modernity itself is a pretty fragile and incomplete invention, to which at one level the post-modern adds little more than illusion and irony.

Because there are other levels than this, however, (post)mod-ernity is still worth exploring, debating. Second time around, I've chosen to highlight some of these dimensions a little more than before. So I have altered very little, except to give a smoother ride to the reader where necessary, but I have added and strengthened sections on globalization, on bodies and the post-human – cyborgs and such – and on the new quest for ethics. I have not explicitly answered my critics but I may have given them a little more to get their teeth into. And when the light shines bright again, we shall all see more clearly what is going on.

Acknowledgements

For the second edition, I gratefully record the critical advice gener-ously given by the following: Deborah Bowen, Tamara Sayers, Bart Simon, Keith Tester, Bill Van Groningen, Ali Zaidi, and Elia Zureik. None agrees with me completely, by any means, and none is responsible for my errors, let alone my intransigence. Faithful are the wounds of friends. Also, I salute the adroit and indispensable secretarial assistance of Joan Westenhaefer. As usual, I cannot but mention family as well. Our children become more critical and more encouraging at the same time. Josh and Miriam helped with specific aspects of popular culture and cyberculture. And although I'll thank her elsewhere, I acknowledge here that for more than a quarter century now, my life partner, Sue, has given steady support and much, much more.

David Lyon, 1998

Introduction: Screen Replicants and Social Realities

This book concerns the postmodern. The concept of postmodernity belongs in social thought because it alerts us to some tremendously important social as well as cultural shifts taking place at the end of the twentieth century. But most people who have encountered the postmodern debate are more aware of the cultural dimension, seen in the arts, architecture and film. So let me start there, with that acme of postmodern movies, *Blade Runner*.

Los Angeles, AD 2019, provides the setting for *Blade Runner*. A group of 'replicants', bio-engineered near-people who normally reside 'off-world', have returned to confront their makers, the high-tech Tyrell corporation. Their complaint is simple; understandably, they object to their four-year lifespan and seek an extension to full human status. Deckard, the 'blade runner', has the unenviable task of tracking these escaped replicants and eliminating or 'retiring' them.

The replicants are not robots, but skin jobs, simulacra. They live fast and furious, if not full, lives. Throughout, they keep appearing in different locations, apparently without having travelled. And they are subjected to testing by humans to determine whether or not they are replicants. One of them, Rachel, produces a photo of her mother, which at last gives a sense that she has a 'real' past, a history, like humans. Deckard finds this enough, evidently, to form an emotional attachment with her, although in the 1992 'Director's Cut' version, this does not culminate in their joint flight to forests and mountains that figured in the earlier version.

The scene of *Blade Runner* is one of urban decay, once grand buildings lying damaged, crowded cosmopolitan streets, endless shopping malls, uncollected garbage and constant grey drizzle. Perhaps the nuclear holocaust has happened already? Undoubtedly, progress is in ruins. Nothing is recognizable as LA; it could be anywhere. Roman and Greek columns, Chinese dragons and Egyptian pyramids are mixed with giant neon ads for Coca-Cola and Pan-Am. Although well-lit transporters flit above the streets, and there are momentary scenes of slick-clean corporate suites, the dominant image is decrepitude, disintegration and a chaotic mishmash of style.

What makes *Blade Runner* postmodern? Let me just mention a limited number of themes that connect with what follows in this book. For a start, 'reality' itself is in question. Replicants want to be 'real' people, but the proof of 'reality', apparently, is a photographic image, a constructed identity. Here is one way of seeing the postmodern: it is a debate about reality. Is the world of solid scientific facts and a purposeful history, bequeathed to us by the European Enlightenment, mere wishful thinking? Or worse, the product of some scheming manipulation of ideas by the powerful? Whatever the case, what are we left with? A quicksand of ambiguity, a *mélange* of artificial images, flickering from the TV screen, or joyful liberation from imposed definitions of 'reality'? Chapter 1 of this book is a reconnaissance mission that charts the postmodern, at least in a preliminary way.

But no sooner do we attempt to describe the postmodern than we find ourselves stumbling over the modern. Vestiges of modernity, residues of progress, seen in buildings and streets, haunt *Blade Runner*. In Chapter 2 I try to summarize some of the key motifs of modernity, especially as perceived by nineteenth- and twentieth-century social thinkers. Revisiting earlier theorists reveals how much they foresaw what we now call 'postmodern'. Karl Marx, for instance, showed how the constant revolutionizing of production meant that 'all that is solid melts into air'. Nothing is immune from the corrosive effects of capitalism. This process persists in the postmodern, where in another replicant's words, experience is 'washed away in time like tears in rain'.

So in a strong sense, this book is also about modernity, despite its title. It must be. For one thing, many themes discussed here under the 'postmodernity' label appear elsewhere as items in a debate about modernity differently designated. For instance, the 'high' modern suggests that modernity has reached a mature phase; 'late', that its days may be numbered; 'hyper', that certain characteristic features of modernity may be exaggerated today; 'meta', that some modern conditions may be transcended; or 'reflexive', that modernity is aware of itself more systematically than ever. According to theorists who use these terms, to describe social conditions as 'postmodern' is premature or misleading or otherwise wrongheaded. And their main complaint is that 'postmodernity' implies that modernity has come to a halt. I have no quarrel with the terms listed, except that I think 'postmodernity' is a somewhat more modest term, suggesting caution about depicting the details of emerging social formations. We shall soon see that in other ways too this book is simultaneously about modernity.

In Chapter 3 another theme emerges, one that also resonates strongly with *Blade Runner*. The modern industrial order seems to give way to new organizing principles structured around knowledge, not Marx's labour and capital, and based on machines to augment mental, rather than muscle power.[1] In the movie, developing knowledge has produced commerce 'more human than human', says Tyrell; genetic engineering introduces human simulacra. The replicants exist in a world that has overcome the limitations of time and space, thanks to the information and communication technologies (CITs) of the 'global village'. What once appeared to some as a seamless shift into an 'information age' is now revealed as a more ambiguous turn. No social, economic or political realities are immune from CIT-related changes, which also stimulate the development of a new cyberculture. Structures of space and place, so characteristic of traditional and modern times, are now supplemented – some say supplanted – by virtual spaces.

But in this 'information age' the old working class has not entirely vanished. Third World peoples, living in LA, form the exploited postindustrial proletariat. Indeed, the idea is challenged that class (or gender, or ethnic difference) is a merely national phenomenon. Production, after all, has been internationalized. No one today buys an automobile made in one country alone. Design decisions may be made, or surveillance data read, in one location, while assembly lines hum, and workers are monitored, in another. Thus the coherence of individual 'societies' is undermined, as global social relations erode an older sense of time and space. Sociology is obliged to go global in its analysis, seeking some sense of how the flows of people, data, images and capital form new patterns. It is this economic, political and cultural mix, enhanced by new media, that gives the postmodern its social referents.

This brings us to the consumer society, where everything is a show, a spectacle, and the public image is all. Some of the female replicants are dressed as models on display. One, Zhora, dies crashing through store-front windows in a seemingly endless arcade. 'Off-world' real estate is advertised, along with the more familiar beers and airlines. Consumerism and consumption are central postmodern motifs, and in Chapter 4 I suggest that they provide pregnant clues about emerging social conditions. We are what we consume. Disneyland turns out to be more real than we thought.

The reality question also impinges directly on humanness. Replicants are near-humans because so many 'human' features have been imported into their constitution that telling the difference is a tease. *Do Androids Dream of Electric Sheep?* is the title of the Phillip K. Dick novel on which *Blade Runner* is based, and this too plays right into the definition-denying question of bodies and humanness, and indeed, takes them a lot further. But the same CITs make it possible to import machine features into human experience and human bodies to such an extent that the conventional limits and characteristics of the body are now in question. Modern anatomy, which encases in skin structures of bone, tissue and flesh, may have to give way to new sense of bodiliness, in which artificial intelligence and virtual reality, genetic engineering and cosmetic surgery reshape the human in strange but subtle ways. The cyborg slips out of *Star Trek* to confront us on the street.

Blade Runner, says Giuliana Bruno,[2] 'posits questions of identity, identification and history in postmodernism'. In Chapter 5 history is foregrounded. What should we do with the (post)modern world? Are we left with only postmodern pastiche, fragments and photos on a collage? Do our self-constructed photofit identities connect us with any bigger story? Can we still discern and work with some essential core of technology or commerce or democracy that survives intact from modernity? Is our 'loss of history' a permanent condition or a temporary amnesia? In fact, the question of history cannot be confronted without also addressing another: that of ethics. The world of the postmodern faces fearsome dilemmas and choices, now made even harder by two things: the vast scale of the issues – the global environment, the future of the human body – and the parallel diminution of ethical resources.[3] In addition, the agony of ethical choice is now more than ever pushed on to individual shoulders. At one level, history offers no hope unless it is linked with communal ethical activity that seeks its source beyond itself. But that is exactly what *Blade Runner*, and with it much post-modern culture, often seems to exclude.

The two versions of *Blade Runner* suggest that the possibilities are not yet closed completely, even though neither seems particularly attractive. The original portrays a bleak and dismal dystopia but leaves residual hints of a 'return to nature'. The 'Director's Cut' version surgically removes even this, leaving us only with increased apocalyptic unease. Are decay and death the terminal postmodern condition? To that last question my answer is no, but not for reasons popular among many postmodern*ists*.

Postmodernity: The History of an Idea

'The blizzard of the world / has crossed the threshold / and . . . has over-
turned / the order of the soul'
Leonard Cohen, 'The Future'

Is postmodernity an idea, a cultural experience, a social condition, or perhaps a combination of all three? Without doubt, postmodernity exists as an idea or a form of critique in the minds of intellectuals and in the media. Since the 1980s it has engendered a huge, sometimes angry, sometimes anxious, debate in many disciplines from geography to theology and from philosophy to political science. This was picked up in the 1990s by more applied disciplines, asking what 'postmodern practice' might mean in management, social work, teaching or law.

The related controversy over 'postmodernism' within the realms of art, architecture, literary and film criticism has raged for somewhat longer. Buildings such as Venturi's National Gallery extension in London, novels such as *The Satanic Verses* or *The English Patient*, and, of course, movies such as *Blade Runner* or *Pulp Fiction* each have been a focus at some point. Inevitably, reference to the postmodern also appears within more popular media, from mocking newsprint dismissal to a three-part series called *The Real Thing* on BBC TV in Britain in the early 1990s. So the postmodern has leaked out well beyond the ivory towers, denoting for many a range of everyday lived experiences.

The idea of postmodernity may yet turn out to be a figment of overheated academic imagination, popular hype, or disappointed radical hopes. It is vulnerable to the criticism that, despite itself, the postmodern could be viewed as a peculiarly western phenomenon, and as such should be rejected in favour of something like 'the global age'.[1] But such objections can be countered, as we shall see. The concept of postmodernity is worth pursuing because it alerts us to a series of highly important questions. It raises our sensitivity and helps us see certain issues as problems to be explained. It obliges us to lift our eyes above narrowly technical and discrete issues and to grapple with historical change on a grand scale. To begin, however, I want to trace socially and intellectually its lineage. What is this idea's history?

A highly significant series of western ideas starts with 'Providence' which is transposed to 'Progress' and shifts from there into 'Nihilism'. Each concept carries some freight of nuanced meaning, but the simple scheme makes a good starting point. Providence refers to God's care for the world after its creation, overseeing the process of history so that it moves forward in a line towards a specific goal. One of its champions was the fourth-century Christian thinker Augustine of Hippo, whose reflections in *The City of God* were to have a deeply shaping effect on western civilization. Providentialism denies any cyclical movement in history, inspiring future-oriented hope rather than resignation or pessimism.[2]

However, the emphasis on history's forward movement was easily combined with the conviction that things were generally improving, especially under the impact of early Enlightenment thought. The wresting of reason from medievalism and tradition prompted many to believe that further and more rapid advance was within human powers to achieve. Ironically, Christian commentators themselves often encouraged this view. But by emphasizing the role of reason and downplaying divine intervention, the seeds were sown for a secular variant of Providence, the idea of Progress.[3] The certainty of our senses supplanted certainty in God's laws and paved the way for the rise of modern scientific world-views. At the same time, Europe was rising to economic and political dominance. As Anthony Giddens says:

> The growth of European power provided, as it were, the material support for the assumption that the new outlook on the world was founded on a firm base which both provided security and offered emancipation from the dogma of tradition.[4]

But how firm was that base?

Although the Enlightenment and thus the modern project were designed to eliminate uncertainty and ambivalence, autonomous reason would always have its doubts. It was bound to if it wished to avoid relapsing into 'dogma'. Relativism of knowledge was built into modern thought. But because in the secular parody of divine thought universal 'laws of nature' were still sought, relativism was viewed as a nuisance. Today's more general acceptance of the view that, however careful our observations, they depend on assumptions, and that those assumptions are connected with world-views and with power positions, makes relativism seem more natural. Those of Nietzschean bent, see here the futility of modern dreams of universalism.[5] The embryo of nihilism started to form in the womb of modernity.

At the height of Victorian confidence, European colonialism and North American frontier settlement, belief in progress reigned supreme. It appeared to be vindicated by (some rather selective noting of) events. Despite what followed – the Great War and the Depression – hopes were not entirely dampened. The Chicago World Fair of 1933 celebrated 'A Century of Progress', and in the same year Hitler came to power promising progress through National Socialism, with its motor cars and medical plans. Faith in Progress flickered following the Second World War, only to be revived artificially by massive scientific and technological development and an unprecedented consumer boom. The concept of modernity came into its own at this time, as a means of encapsulating these changes. But the damage was done. Colonialism crumbled as political independence was granted to state after state, and peoples migrated from one part of the world to another at increasing rates. The downside of industrialism became fearfully apparent in the degradation of the environment, the depletion of unrenewable resources, and the deterioration of the ozone layer.

The result, at more than a merely intellectual level, was a massive questioning of received doctrines. In the western world a tremendous cultural upheaval loosened or uprooted older boundary markers. The 1960s presented both political and cultural challenges of immense importance: tradition and taste were up for grabs. The 'expressive revolution' was unleashed.[6] New social movements sprang up. Cynicism was fuelled by Vietnam and then by Watergate. Paralleling these developments, democracy movements budded in Eastern Europe that would flower in the disintegration of communism. The years 1789–1989 thus became the symbolic two centuries span of modernity, expressed politically as the quest for a rationalized world – from the French Revolution to the fall of bureaucratic state socialism.

With the grandiose dreams of westernization tarnished, and the rise of oppositional voices such as Sunni Islam,[7] the idea of universal knowledge or culture was queried with greater intensity than ever. Progress through technological development and economic growth appeared as at best a mixed blessing. Reason brought as many nightmares as sweet dreams and the irrationalisms of drugs or new religions seemed to promise better. Political legitimation and citizen-worker motivation seemed at low ebb. Intellectuals squabbled over whether this was crisis as catastrophe or as opportunity, and sought for new terms to describe the emerging situation. 'Postmodernity' is one such term, which has to be set alongside preferences for alternative prefixes to 'modernity', or other concepts, such as globalization, that do not overtly refer to the modern.

It is a simplified, though not simplistic, scheme that charts the course from Providence to Progress and from there to Nihilism. Of course, one can object that nihilism has ancient roots, or that providentialists and progressivists are alive and well today. Equally, one can observe that shallow as well as serious versions of each concept exist. The former may suggest that Providentialism is little more than fatalism; progressivism is always blindly optimistic; and nihilism completely careless, irresponsible. But in terms of trying to grasp immense shifts in cultural sensibility, which both inspire and echo tectonic social forces, this scheme highlights emerging moods. If the postmodern mood exhibits nihilistic tendencies then this means that reality is blurred and that establishing truth is not as straightforward as it once seemed. It does not necessarily mean that people believe in nothing or that they are paralysed by the senselessness of existence.

As used here, the postmodern refers above all to the exhaustion – but not necessarily to the demise – of modernity. As a rough analytic device it is worth distinguishing between postmodern*ism*, when the accent is on the cultural, and postmodern*ity*, when the emphasis is on the social.[8] I say 'rough' for reasons that will be explained more fully below. Simply put, they lie in the impossibility of *separating* the cultural from the social, however desirable the *distinction* might be. There is a strong sense in which the social has become more cultural.

'Postmodernism', refers here to cultural and intellectual phenomena, to the production, consumption and distribution of symbolic goods. Intellectually, one example is the forsaking of 'foundationalism', the view that science is built on a firm base of observable facts, in the philosophy of science. This escalated into the so-called 'science wars' of the 1990s. Beyond this, postmodernism questions all the key commitments of the European Enlightenment. As Gary Woller says, 'postmodernism is about deposing the trinity of the Enlightenment – reason, nature and progress – which presumably triumphed over the earlier Trinity'.[9] But in everyday life, the postmodern may be seen in the blurring of boundaries between 'high' and 'low' culture; the collapse of hierarchies of knowledge, taste and opinion; and the interest in the local rather than the universal. If science is soft, its authority is dethroned. 'Learn from Las Vegas' (or from natives, or nature) becomes the slogan. Beyond this lies the loss of 'logocentrism' in the proliferation of discourses; the printed book and the TV screen, word and image, text and figure.

'Postmodernity', on the other hand, while still concentrating on the exhaustion of modernity, has to do with putative social changes. Certain features of modernity are being inflated, and by contrast shrink others into insignificance, to yield new social configurations. While still recognizable to those familiar with modernity, the reshaped conditions call for reappraisal. The old organizational thrust of modernity, argues one group, is jeopardized by the rampant differentiation and fragmentation of the present.[10] Either a new kind of society is coming into being, whose contours can already be perceived dimly (Zygmunt Bauman's view), or a new stage of capitalism is being inaugurated (David Harvey's position). In both cases, previous modes of social analysis and political practice are called in question, as power balances shift and ties are unbound and re-bound. And in both cases, two issues are crucial: the prominence of new information and communication technologies, facilitating further extensions of social relationships such as globalization; and consumerism, perhaps eclipsing the conventional centrality of production.

In the end, however, postmodern*ism* cannot be understood without postmodern*ity*, any more than the cultural makes sense without the social and vice versa. Postmodern debates have reopened the question of how the cultural and the social imbricate with and inform each other. To understand social change, as the best commentators have always argued, one has to understand cultural change.[11] At the same time, this book stops well short of identifying the cultural with the social, or of collapsing the one into the other. The power relations and interdependencies that characterize the social field may not simply be grasped by concepts like 'society' or 'the social', but neither is their meaning exhausted by reference to culture. That social field is understood here as touching upon the economy and the nation state, on ethnicity, region, gender and class.

The progenitors

In order to understand the main currents of postmodern thought it helps to step back and interrogate those thinkers who anticipated postmodernity. Undoubtedly the single most significant figure is Friedrich Nietzsche (1844–1900), a postmodern *avant la lettre*. He announced in 1888 that 'nihilism stands at the door'. This, the 'uncanniest of all guests' was indeed eyed suspiciously and with some trepidation in Europe. But for Nietzsche, truth was 'only the solidification of old metaphors'. This had to be understood in the context of the Europe of the Enlightenment. The metaphors must be melted again to reveal them as human belief and the opinion of this or that social group. He devoted his days to exposing the hollowness of Enlightenment hopes. But his work has only come home, with a vengeance, a century later.[12]

One of the most basic themes of postmodern debate revolves around reality, or lack of reality, or multiplicity of realities. Nihilism is the Nietzschean concept corresponding most closely to this fluid and anchorless sense of reality.[13] When the restless doubting attitude of modern reason turns on reason itself, nihilism results. Rationality, whether in art, philosophy or in science, is attacked by nihilism. So-called systems of reason, asserts Nietzsche, are actually systems of persuasion. Thus claims to have discovered truth are unmasked as what Nietzsche called the 'will to power'. Those making such claims place themselves above those to whom the claims are made, thus dominating them.

Nietzsche achieved notoriety for proclaiming the 'death of God'. Though some take this merely as a trope for the loss of philosophical foundations, arguably it also represents serious anti-theism. At any rate, Nietzsche's slogan 'the death of God' means that we can no longer be sure of anything. Morality is a lie, truth is fiction. The Dionysian option of accepting nihilism, of living with no illusions or pretence, but doing so enthusiastically, joyfully, is all that remains. Following from this, nothing is left of the difference between truth and error; it is mere delusion. No guarantee of grounds for difference – such as God – remain beyond our language and its concepts. Difference is also revealed as part of the will to power, a point that connects Nietzsche's thought with that of Heidegger, to whom we shall turn in a moment.

While cosmic traumas such as the death of God may seem somewhat abstract and ethereal, it should be noted that a generation before Nietzsche, Karl Marx (1818–83) viewed the same process in a much more mundane light. What Nietzsche saw as a predicament for science, rationality and metaphysics, Marx attributed to the 'banal everyday workings of the bourgeois economic order'.[14] In other words, under capitalism people allow the market to organize life, including our inner lives. By equating everything with its market value – commodifying – we end up seeking answers to questions about what is worthwhile, honourable, and even what is real, in the marketplace. Nihilism can also be understood in this practical, everyday sense.

In the postmodern context, Marx and Engels' adaptation of Prospero's words in *The Tempest*, 'All that is solid melts into air', have become the new favoured text quoted from *The Communist Manifesto*.[15] Interestingly enough, on Prospero's lips the solidity of everyday life, including human life itself, is an appearance that must give way before a larger reality. For the postmodernized Marx, supposedly solid realities dissolve in the bath of bourgeois acids, decomposing meaning and reality themselves. In Nietzsche's nihilism, the reversal is complete. The lack of a 'larger reality' is for him the start of life without illusions.

A second character in the prehistory of postmodernity is Martin Heidegger (1889–1976). Most famous for his 1927 book, *Being and Time*, Heidegger was concerned above all with the nature of thought in existing human beings. From his reading of Brentano, Dostoevsky and Kierkegaard he concluded that attending to concrete and relevant historical problems showed the way forward for philosophy. These other figures grappled with the same set of existential questions as Nietzsche, though they came to different conclusions.

Dostoevsky wrestled with the issue of whether one could claim that 'since there is no God, everything is permitted', while Kierkegaard sought authentic human existence in relation to God, which he saw as an ongoing quest of faith and commitment. Like Heidegger, these two tried to face the challenge of the modern world, expressed in the dominance of natural science and the rise of technology, which seemed to squeeze out concern with real-life individuals.[16]

Heidegger shares Nietzsche's interest in 'philosophy of difference', but also goes beyond Nietzsche in declaring that Being, not truth, is what should concern philosophers. Heidegger disputes Nietzsche's assertion that difference is just a product of the will to power. 'Being' is prior to all the many 'beings' we encounter on earth, including humans. So it is not our human wills, but Being itself that produces difference. The mistake of philosophers, including Nietzsche, is to focus on truth in exploring the relationship between beings. Their prior existence should rather be the central concern.

Today, humanism finds itself in crisis precisely because it replaces God with humanity at the centre of the universe, says Heidegger. Humans take themselves to be the measure of all things rather than recognizing the difference of Being. In this sense, humanism is not opposed to technology. On the contrary, technology expresses the controlling, dominating approach that comes from putting humans at the centre of things. 'The essence of technology is not something technological', insists Heidegger. Acknowledging this is the only escape route from the clutches of modern technological constraint.

For Heidegger, the way forward is to come to terms with our condition; neither metaphysics nor humanism nor technology will do as a basis for life. This 'coming to terms with' (as opposed to 'overcoming') Heidegger summarized in the word *Verwindung*. Such an approach is followed in the debate over postmodernity by Gianni Vattimo in particular, who resists the apocalyptic effusions of some who see the end of modernity as decadent decline and cultural collapse. Heidegger sees a 'twilight' in western thought, but regards it as an opportunity for reconstruction, not a terminus.

There is no point pretending that these giants of so-called existential thought were not engaged in a search for a post-Christian basis for interpreting history. As Vattimo says:

> Only modernity, in developing and elaborating in strictly worldly and secular terms the Judeo-Christian heritage – i.e., the idea of history as

the history of salvation, articulated in terms of creation, sin, redemption, and waiting for the Last Judgement – gives ontological weight to history and a determining sense to our position within it.[17]

The question raised by Heidegger, and, for that matter, Kierkegaard, is whether the critique of the old foundations locks us into a purely secular alternative.[18] This question is raised with increasing sharpness as the twentieth gives way to the twenty-first century. Social theorists such as Donna Haraway and David Noble acknowledge historically, but discard definitively, the Christian themes and threads woven into the fabric of modernity.[19]

The selfsame question lurks within a third account of the 'tragedy of culture', that of Georg Simmel (1858–1918). Now widely recognized not merely as a founding father of sociology, but also as the 'sole postmodern thinker' among them,[20] Simmel straddles the worlds of sociology and cultural analysis. This tragedy, or crisis of culture, was for him the widening gap between the objective culture, seen in technology for instance, and the increasingly alienated individual, frustrated in the quest for genuine individuality. Simmel began his analysis not, like so many modernistic sociologists, with some grand total view of society, but with the fragments of social reality.

Simmel's sociology of culture emphasizes the apparent loss of meaning in the modern world of industrialism, a loss that he associated with, among other things, the 'decline of Christianity'. He regarded contemporary movements such as socialism in politics or impressionism in art as the response to a felt need for a 'final object' in life, 'above everything relative, above the fragmentary character of human existence'.[21] But in his own diagnosis of modernity he tried to paint a picture of the 'passing moment' of life, in all its seeming disconnectness and dissonance.

For Simmel, the social experiences of modernity were especially strongly felt in the growing urban metropolis and in the alienation of a mature money economy.[22] And they were best understood in terms of the inner lives of individuals, thus providing a sort of social psychological counterpoint to Marx's analysis of capitalist society. Simmel prefigured some of the central discussions of postmodernity.[23] Unlike Marx, Simmel sees the sphere of circulation, exchange and consumption as relatively autonomous, a law to itself. It is the symbolic significance of money and commodities that fascinates

Simmel. The growing attachment to this 'world of things' steadily devalues the human world.

Simmel also commented on what he saw as the autonomy of the cultural sphere. As objective culture – form – increasingly militates against life, Simmel develops a tragic vision in which for instance, marriage becomes merely oppressive and lifeless, or religion loses contact with distinct beliefs and degenerates into mysticism. And lastly, the aesthetic is accented. For Simmel himself, art was a means of overcoming the contradictions of modernity, and he believed that in times of confusion and uncertainty a more general shift towards the aesthetic would occur. Both these motifs, noting the withdrawal from form, and seeking meaning or even morality in art, reappear in the debate over postmodernity.

The new luminaries

With some of the 'pre-postmodern' pieces of the puzzle in place we can start to see the postmodern picture more clearly. Like the history of ideas, however, the jigsaw puzzle metaphor itself would be objectionable to some postmodern theorists. The very notion that we can build up progressively towards a complete or – heaven help us – total view of postmodernity would be anathema. Almost by definition, too, the concept of postmodernity is geographically dispersed, so its 'history' migrates. While some European thinkers help spark postmodern debate, they often have American connections, and the USA, after all, epitomizes the 'modernity' from which postmodernity derives. All I am claiming, to change metaphors, is that we can identify the streams feeding into the postmodern river, not that we can exhaustively analyse, let alone tame, the river itself.

Although I shall identify these streams in terms of some specific authors, a common theme, picked up from the last section and amplified in what follows, concerns knowledge and discourse. Nietzsche's multiple realities are each articulated as 'discourses' and reappear strongly, for instance, in the work of Jacques Derrida. Derrida has been misread popularly as saying that no meaning exists beyond language; discourse is severed from the world. This highly influential reading goes on like this: with no God to guarantee them, signifiers float free, to be understood only in relation to one another, seen in different discourses. Like ice floes on the river

during spring break-up, the world of meaning fractures and fragments, making it hard even to speak of meaning as traditionally
conceived.

It is true, of course, that time-honoured ways of thinking about
knowledge evaporate, to be reconstituted as constructed surfaces
or – as seen most clearly in Foucault's work – in relation to power.
The very possibility of acquiring knowledge or of giving an account
of the world is called in question. Whereas once one could observe
how the structure of knowledge reflected the structure of the
society that produced it – think of Max Weber's studies of bureaucracy in rationalizing Germany – the postmodern denies such structure in either knowledge or society. Farewell to knowledge as once
construed; welcome instead to circulating, pliable discourses.

The term 'postmodern' came into popular usage above all after
Jean-François Lyotard's *The Postmodern Condition* appeared.[24]
Once established, however, other – mainly French – authors were
also associated with this tendency. During the 1980s, and despite
the fact that several of these discarded, denied or distanced themselves from the term, the postmodern came to be linked with their
names. Most prominent within this debate are Jean Baudrillard,
Jacques Derrida, Michel Foucault and of course Lyotard himself.
To simplify matters I shall refer mainly to them, although others,
such as Gilles Deleuze, Gianni Vattimo and Richard Rorty, cannot
be ignored. Simplicity also dictates that we focus on one or two relevant ideas of each author so that when I refer to them later the
reader will not have too hard a time disentangling the threads.

'Simplifying to the extreme,' says Lyotard, 'I define *postmodern*
as incredulity towards metanarratives.'[25] Innocently posing as a
report on the status of knowledge in the advanced societies for the
Conseil des Universités de Québec, Lyotard's book plunges right
into the fate of Enlightenment thought in an age of globalized high
technology. The main 'metanarrative' in question follows the
Enlightenment line that science legitimates itself as the bearer of
emancipation. *Modern* knowledge justifies itself in relation to
grand narratives such as wealth creation or workers' revolution. We
will be freed as we understand our world better. Lyotard knocks
the bottom out of this by his claim that we can no longer fall back
on such discourses. Why not?

Science, once taken to be the touchstone of legitimate knowledge, has lost its assumed unity. As science spawns disciplines and

sub-disciplines it becomes harder to maintain that they are all part of the same enterprise. Each form of discourse is forced to generate what home-made authority it can. Scientists must be much more modest than hitherto; so far from stating definitively how things are, only opinions can be offered. As Zygmunt Bauman puts it, intellectuals no longer legislate, they just interpret.[26] All that remains is 'flexible networks of language games'.[27] The traditional sense of 'knowledge' thus decomposes. Lyotard does not explore in any depth the sociological aspects of his argument, though he does refer to some economic and political factors that affect the status of knowledge.

The growing field of Science and Technology Studies has taken insights like Lyotard's much further, in an attempt to understand the growth of knowledge as a social and cultural process. The field embraces everything from macro-level studies of, say, the military shaping of major technoscience projects, through to micro-scale analyses of how scientific decisions about how to proceed are actually reached within the laboratory. Such social influences turn out to be profound, subverting the sense that some sciences are as 'hard' as their proponents claim. The success of such studies can be marred, however, by overstatement, suggesting that no external world exists, or that the whole process of doing science is in the end radically subjective.

Although the seeds of delegitimation were sown during the nineteenth century, when, for example, Nietzsche turned the truth requirement of science back on itself, for Lyotard, the harvest has been ripened by the advent of computer technologies in the later twentieth century. These have helped shift the emphasis to 'performativity', the efficiency and productivity of systems, and away from the issues of intrinsic value or purposes of knowledge. Computer printouts are trusted as indicators of 'reliable' data and become the guide for styles of research and investigation. Indeed, Lyotard observes that the rationales or purposes of knowledge are seldom sought beyond the immediate. 'Who needs metanarratives when management will do?' might be asked by those who have not yet woken up to the dissolution of the 'metanarratives' themselves.

This is linked with another post-war development: the resurgence of liberal capitalism, 'a renewal that has eliminated the communist alternative and valorized the individual enjoyment of goods and services'.[28] In one phrase Lyotard thus points out how the collapse of communism as an ideology (and, after 1989, as a political system) further clears the way for the 'atomization of the social', this time into consumer clusters of taste and fashion, a theme we shall pursue in a moment. First, however, it is worth commenting that the collapse of communism is of more than passing interest to Lyotard, for whom the future of Marxism is a vital aspect of the postmodern question. Marxism, after all, represents one of the grandest metanarratives ever. For Lyotard, while Marxist analysis retains some of its relevance – computer-generated information itself is now a commodity – he acknowledges that Marxism has lost forever its claim to universality.

If for Lyotard the atomization of the social means we are each bound up in our local language games, for Jacques Derrida it is a question of 'texts'. Like Lyotard, however, Derrida raises crucial queries concerning what he calls the western philosophical tradition. Cultural life involves texts we produce, says Derrida, intersecting with other texts that influence ours in ways we cannot ever unravel. The task of 'deconstruction', a strategy gleaned from Derrida's reading of Heidegger, is to raise persistent questions about our own texts and those of others, to deny that any text is settled or stable. The logocentric stance of modernity is radically disrupted by stressing the indeterminacy of language. Though some, such as Richard Rorty, take Derrida to be arguing that the modern era of Enlightenment is over, others insist that he should be seen as still working within those parameters.[29]

Whether or not Derrida would accept that his is a postmodern account, it is certainly the case that his concept of deconstruction has entered the canon – forgive me! – of postmodern critique. Just as Lyotard's description shows how scientists have lost status, so Derrida's indicates how authority itself has waned. Literally, the 'authors' of texts – any cultural artefacts – cannot impose their own meanings on their texts when they are clearly not their sole product. And once the text is out in the open, it is extended by others' interpretations, spiralling endlessly beyond all efforts that might be made to tether the text to truth or to fix its meaning in place. It is interesting that while some take this to mean that all knowledge is contingent, or that agreement on meaning is impossible, Derrida himself strives to ensure that his own texts accurately reflect his views and that interviewers do not misunderstand him.

The deconstructive mode may be applied elsewhere, as a way of viewing distrust of tradition, or the free play of desire. Popular participation in cultural production becomes more of an option in this view, such that texts are reworked and recombined by their consumers. Collage becomes the postmodern style. TV soap opera audiences are polled for their preferred episode outcomes. Colonial, ranch and row houses sit together in the suburbs. Scott Joplin, Georg Telemann, Mahalia Jackson, Sting, Igor Stravinsky and Joni Mitchell meet on the radio. But lest this process be thought of merely as a kind of cheerful democratization (that is, Disneyfication) of culture, some critics warn that mass-market manipulation is an equally likely outcome.[30]

Nietzsche's 'truth' as merely the 'solidification of old metaphors' is but a short step away from Derrida's contingent world of textuality. Boundaries between knowledge and world, or text and interpretation, no longer exist; the mind is always renewing and redefining the texts it tries to contain. This implies that science can no longer presume on logical coherence or the discoverability of truth. This includes social science, of course, long riven by disputes over positivist and hermeneutic – interpretive – approaches. The conclusion drawn by Bauman for sociology is that it simply has to accept its 'insider' status, not attempting to 'correct' laypersons' views but trying to discover opportunities such study offers.[31] But while it may be granted that more modesty would not be amiss, sociology would cease to exist if all sense of critique were corroded away.

Other inferences have been drawn especially from Derrida's work by feminists, notably Luce Irigaray, for whom the issue of *women* and language is central. Debates have raged following Irigaray's work, over whether or not a unique women's language exists. Derrida defends *différance* against the tyranny of sameness, and wants to deconstruct the male–female dichotomy. But Irigaray apparently harks back to the dichotomy in claiming feminine subjectivity as a means of empowerment.[32] The feminist debate with the postmodern – represented in France by others such as Julia Kristeva and Hélène Cixous, and in North America by figures such as Judith Butler – is a highly significant one, to which I return in Chapters 5 and 6.

Riding on what are in many ways parallel tracks, Michel Foucault's work touches on themes similar to Derrida's. But while Derrida focuses on the literary and the philosophical, Foucault refers more to the human sciences. I hinted a moment ago that the very notion of a 'history of ideas' would be unacceptable to most postmodern theorists. To suggest a linear progression of concepts and to explore the connection between each in terms of their antecedents is a hopelessly modernist enterprise. For Foucault, building on Nietzsche, *genealogy* is rather what should be pursued. Knowledge is still in question, but linked with – or melded with – power and also with bodies. In genealogy, a line of descent is traced, but no causal connections are assumed and no origins are sought. Whereas for Nietzsche the body could be used to explain behaviour, Foucault, in his early work at least, thinks of bodies as being worked upon. There, bodies are passive.[33]

In Foucault's scheme, two main *epistemes* – as he calls them – may be discerned in western thought. Neo-Classical thought, dating from the seventeenth century, had no special place for human beings. But the modern *episteme*, on the other hand, characterizing the nineteenth century onwards, actually constitutes 'man' as both object and subject. As language becomes detached from representation, and as the 'natural' gives way to the 'normal' so the distinctive possibilities of the human sciences are born.[34] But if their birth can be traced, then, by the same token, so can their death. Foucault exposes what he sees as the deep limitations of sociology and psychology and shows how humans may also be 'unmade' by disciplines such as psychoanalysis. His work lent strong credence not only to the idea that the modern *episteme* was crumbling, but that its object – 'Man' – was dead.

Foucault's later writings underscore this stark conclusion, but from different angles. While the human sciences – and their applied counterparts such as social work – might be seen as 'discourses of power', locating, tabulating, classifying, processing us within alien schemes, this is all the more evident in regimes of sexual repression and prison life that Foucault also analysed. The strong impression given by his study of the Panopticon penitentiary architecture, for instance, is that we are all manipulated by power, like prisoners, yet colluding with our own incarceration in society. Human beings, in the sense of conscious, active, even rebellious creatures, indeed appear pretty well dead in this account.[35] For the Foucault of *Discipline and Punish*, freedom seems like a figment of modernist philosophy. On the other hand, by focusing on the apparent unfreedoms of modernity, Foucault pushes us towards the paradox that the postmodern problem may be a surfeit of freedom, or at least, too many choices.[36]

If Foucault offers few clues about what might lie beyond, his compatriot Jean Baudrillard offers even less. Indeed, he advises us to 'forget Foucault'.[37] What he does offer shifts the spotlight once more, this time to the media of modern communication. Whereas earlier eras depended either on face-to-face symbolic exchanges or, in the modern period, print, the contemporary world is dominated by images from the electronic mass media. Immediate communication takes place over vast distances unimaginable to dwellers in traditional societies, and takes the form of montage – piecing together for effect – which distinguishes it from print. In the process, our understanding of reality is radically revised.[38]

Along with several other postmodern thinkers, Baudrillard's work is forged in part out of a debate with the ghost of Karl Marx. Near the centre of the storm of student revolt in 1968, he was then involved with anarchism, structural Marxism and media theory. But in *The Consumer Society* his work clearly split away from orthodox Marxism in its emphasis on consumption as the overriding feature of class domination. Within monopoly capitalism people are mobilized as consumers; 'their needs become as essential as their labour power'.[39] Commodity exchange is not unimportant, he said, but the *symbolic* exchange of the consumer order represents the real basis of radical critique of capitalism.[40]

How, then, can such a critique be mounted? Certainly not on the basis of Marxist 'foundations' or the rationalist idea that concepts can somehow grasp their object. These are, in Lyotard's terms, fallen metanarratives. Now, says Baudrillard, our situation is one of 'hyperreality'. With distinctions dissolved between objects and their representations, we are left only with 'simulacra'. These refer to nothing but themselves. Media messages, such as TV ads, are prime examples. This self-referentiality goes far beyond Max Weber's fears for a disenchanted, detraditionalized world. Signs lose contact with things signified; in some advertisements the object, whether car, watch or beer bottle, no longer appears. The late twentieth century is witness to unprecedented evaporation of the grounds for meaning. The quest for some division between the real and the unreal, or even the true and untrue, moral and immoral, is futile.

Despite Baudrillard's provocative prose – some think it absurd –

it is difficult not to grant that he seems to be on to something. The world of TV, and especially of virtual reality, does simulate increasingly well, such that the difference fades between the erstwhile 'real' and the 'virtual'. What is experienced in virtual reality environments is real enough for those wired up with headsets and sensors, just as a dream is real to the dreamer or a psychosomatic ailment is real enough to the sufferer. So the simulation, as Baudrillard insists, is not a fake or a falsehood, and it certainly has real enough effects. But it does make a mockery of old markers of meaning. As Alain Touraine admits, at least Baudrillard is honest about the loss of social references.[41] Still, one might be forgiven for asking whether this perspective dissolves altogether the last traces of the 'social'. Baudrillard believes that the 'social' has disappeared in the cracks between instrumentality (corporations and governments, working in markets) and culture (meaning is just subjective, unshareable). In the latter realm, the quest for meaning revolves increasingly around identity.[42] But is Baudrillard right? And can this count as critique?

It would appear that the very term 'critique' loses its salience when there is no position from which to assess, evaluate, judge. Yet more than one social theorist sees Baudrillard's ideas – albeit with the apocalyptic volume turned down several degrees – as potentially fruitful for just such social critique.[43] Others, admittedly, think he so recklessly overstates his case – that everything can be understood in terms of the TV simulacra, or that in our meaningless digitalized societies melancholy is the norm – that critique is impossible without more radically modifying his stance.[44] Yet others, such as Arthur Kroker, pick up his 'panic' as the 'key psychological mood of postmodern culture', marked by its *fin de millénaire* swings from deep euphoria to deep despair.[45]

Perhaps what this really indicates is that Baudrillard's own quest for the real is not over. The world of pure simulacra, of apocalyptic artificiality is seen most clearly in Baudrillard's searing study of *America*. Its hyperreal setting, a highway in the desert, supposedly sums up American civilization. Some things, he affirms, simply cannot be exported, so the nostalgia of many American intellectuals towards European ideas and culture is pointless. But Europeans are not without nostalgia, in this case for failed revolutions. Perhaps, Bryan Turner hints, a 'submerged religious paradigm' lingers on here that makes Baudrillard not just postmodern, but *anti*-modern. Maybe 'his own work can be read as a quest for the real, which disappears before his eyes like a mirage in the desert'.[46]

The social and the cultural

While aspects of my whirlwind tour of the career of postmodernity may be unfamiliar to some working in the social sciences, what I have tried to show is that the social and the cultural are tightly intertwined. Debates over the future direction of social – and global – trends cannot afford to ignore their cultural dimensions. The social realm may not be disappearing, but it is undergoing radical change, in the direction of what Manuel Castells calls the 'network society'. Paralleling this is the rise of identity as a source of meaning and the crucible of culture. But it is equally myopic to imagine that any solid understanding of contemporary art, architecture or film may be obtained without some sense of social, political, and economic changes occurring at the turn of the twenty-first century.

The way that Providence was transposed into Progress and from there gave birth to Nihilism did not happen in an intellectual vacuum. The history of capitalist development, of the growth of science and technology, along with later crises of both capitalism and industrialism help us understand how these ideas were carried, obscured, or given their moment. Similarly, these ideas have themselves been potent influences in inspiring hopeful action or in instilling a sense of resignation and complacency. And this is exactly why some commentators are so critical of postmodern ideas: the clash occurs at a profound level.

Marshall Berman, for instance, wonders why people would ever want to choke with Foucault in his prison. He suggests that Foucault offers an excuse for escapism among middle-aged radical refugees from the 1960s student-worker movements. What's the point of resisting injustice when 'even our dreams of freedom only add more links to our chains'? But, 'once we grasp the total futility of it all, at least we can relax'.[47] Berman's irritation with Foucault echoes the view that unless class struggle is prioritized you must be resigned to injustice. For Foucault, as for many postmodern critics, the problem of modernity encompasses, but is deeper than, capitalism. So much so, I shall argue, that solutions may not ultimately be sought where Marx sought them, within modernity.

We can see how the major motifs of postmodern thought also link the social and the cultural. The notion that modernity must be rethought, revised or rejected is not unconnected with actual social conditions created in the wake of proliferating computer and screen-centred technologies or the conquests wrought by consumer capitalism. The global culture facilitated by the spread of electronic technologies, for instance, does much to relativize once-dominant western ideas, while the same technologies also enable us to mix-and-match musical tastes or to channel-hop with the TV remote. The forsaking of foundationalism in science and the erosion of hierarchies of knowledge and opinion seem much less surprising or arcane in this light.

Nonetheless, big questions remain. The postmodern may refer to the exhaustion of modernity but does this invite obituaries or merely a call to make room for a fresh appraisal of modernity? Is logocentrism dead or dormant? Would we fall into the trap of modern linear logic if we imagined that the path from Providence to Progress and from thence to Nihilism is a one-way street with no return? However we respond to these questions, they will not fully be faced by focusing merely on either supposed social changes alone or cultural shifts alone. The social sciences, though they began by trying to isolate factors implicit in social change, on the model of the natural sciences, increasingly take their cues from cultural analysis. This does not mean abandoning the quest for systematic investigation. Rather, it spells the filling out of such investigation by its integration with cultural analysis. Postmodernism and postmodernity must each be viewed in terms of the other.

Modernity and its Discontents

'They paved paradise / and put up a parking lot'
Joni Mitchell, 'Big Yellow Taxi'

Notions parading as novelties usually have a past. Modernity, though a relative newcomer on the conceptual scene, has actually been around a long time, under other names. But the arrival of 'postmodernity' forces us to ask, well, what is or was modernity? Like postmodernity, the concept of modernity has a long history. In the fifth century, the Latin term *modernus* was used to distinguish the official Christian present from the pagan Roman past.[1] But the French Enlightenment established the term more in the way we use it today. The *philosophes* declared that a dispute between the *anciens* and *modernes* was being resolved in favour of the latter. Modern, post-medieval civilization, based supremely on Reason, was superior.

So what is modernity? The term refers to the social order that emerged following the Enlightenment. Though its roots may be traced further back, the modern world is marked by its unprecedented dynamism, its dismissal or marginalizing of tradition, and by its global consequences. Time seemed to speed up, and space to open up. Modernity's forward-looking thrust relates strongly to belief in progress and the power of human reason to produce freedom. But its discontents spring from the same source: unrealized optimism and the inherent doubt fostered by post-traditional thought. These, along with the unintended effects of classifying, ordering and rationalizing modern life, clipped freedom's wings.

Though modernity can be seen in achievements such as science and technology or democratic politics, it also affects profoundly the routines of everyday life. 'Who says?' – authority questions, and 'Who am I?' – identity questions – are posed in new and urgent ways.

As sociology developed during the nineteenth century, the idea, though not the concept, of modernity was strongly present. The concept of modernity itself achieved prominence only recently. Although 'modernization' frequently featured as a means of summing up the social and political processes associated with technology-led economic growth, modernity itself – as the cumulative consequences of those processes – was a term not widely in use before the 1970s. Unlike the concept of capitalism, which originated in Europe, modernity is associated much more with the USA. In the work of Peter Berger, for instance, modernity means the whole constellation of characteristics typical of 'modern' societies, and he questions how far this could be exported to countries that had not yet thus developed.[2] Previous dominant assumptions included the view that modernization was a kind of inevitable and desirable process which simply required the right set of factors. 'Underdeveloped' countries could thus be 'developed' by more or less following a formula that looked suspiciously western.

In W. W. Rostow's famous (mid-twentieth-century) metaphor, only when certain conditions were met, a set of criteria fulfilled, would any given country have gathered enough momentum for 'take-off' into modernity.[3] There would, for instance, have to be mechanical assistance for labour, and dependence on inanimate energy sources for power. The labour market would have to exist, and workers would be supervised under one roof. Moreover the all-important 'entrepreneur' would have to appear. In Daniel Lerner's account of *The Passing of Traditional Society* the entrepreneur, the grocer of Balgat, appeared as hero.[4] By acting as intermediary between foreign traders from more commercially advanced societies and the rural peasants of Turkey, and by having the first radio receiver in his store, he acted as the harbinger of modernity.

Berger's work, however, looked at modernity not just as an economic, political and technological affair but as a profoundly cultural one. His studies, like those of Marx, Weber, Durkheim and Simmel before him, recognized that questions of religion and culture are crucial to understanding modernity and what preceded it. The

question then becomes the classic sociological one of how tradition
was eroded and broken up by the coming of modernity. Tradition,
in turn, is the set of rules given by the village community, religious
and cultic life, or the elders or kings who held sway. Modernity
replaces such rules, with their taken-for-granted character, with
new ones relating to the routines of factory life or the regulations
of the bureaucratic organization. Disturbing daily routines of
timing and spacing raises in turn questions of authority and identity.

How did modernity attempt to answer these questions? Modernity is all about the massive changes that took place at many
levels from the mid-sixteenth century onwards, changes signalled
by the shifts that uprooted agricultural workers and transformed
them into mobile industrial urbanites. Modernity questions all conventional ways of doing things, substituting authorities of its own,
based in science, economic growth, democracy or law. And it un-
settles the self: if identity is given in traditional society, in modernity
it is constructed. Modernity started out to conquer the world in the
name of Reason; certainty and social order were to be founded on
new bases. For about two centuries it seemed that this vision would
be vindicated. So why do many now see modernity as its own
gravedigger?

Modernity's achievement

The achievement of modernity is astonishing. In the space of a few
decades a transformation began in Europe that would alter the
world in unprecedented and irreversible ways. Much of what we
now take for granted as 'normal' aspects of everyday life would
have been unthinkable to my great grandmother, let alone to hers.
While my grandmother rode in a car – a Morris Cowley to be precise – and used the telephone, her mother was more familiar with
steam trains and the telegraph. Her mother, in turn, relied on
horses for transport, though she did witness the birth of the postage
stamp for letter communication. For all these women, space travel
was the stuff of science fiction *à la* Jules Verne or H. G. Wells, and
satellite communication or cloning simply unthought of.

Lest the reader think I am lapsing into some sort of technological
determinism, let me say quickly that profound social changes are
involved in each of these innovations. The routines of everyday life

are altered, for instance, when we no longer have to rely on face-to-face relationships in order to communicate. Our social relations become stretched over time and space, connected by tissues of TV signals and fibre-optic cables. More and more, we do things at a distance. The little paths we trace between dawn and dusk are quite different if timetables, clocks and computers rather than seasons, sunrise and nightfall frame our coming and going. Even 'dawn and dusk' are less meaningful concepts when activities can continue uninterrupted by the loss of natural light. Artificial electric light simply takes over, and we come to depend on it doing so.

But not only are the consequences of such technical developments deeply social, the causes are as well. The most conspicuous motor driving them is capitalism, with its constant quest for new raw materials, new sources of labour power and, more recently, new technologies to supplement or replace that labour power and new applications that might attract new consumers. From the start, one innovation spawned another. Speeding up one part of the process, say, wool combing, created shortages or bottlenecks in another, for which some novel technique was sought. As Karl Marx noted in *The Communist Manifesto*,

> The bourgeoisie cannot exist without constantly revolutionizing the instruments of production, and with them the relations of production, and with them all the relations of society . . . Constant revolutionizing of production, uninterrupted disturbance of all social relations, ever-lasting uncertainty and agitation, distinguish the bourgeois epoch from all earlier ones.

In this phrase Marx catches the *societal* scope of the changes taking place, changes that others have limited by terms such as 'industrialization'. In truth, while 'modernity' may seem a rather vague term, it does have the virtue of indicating the sheer magnitude of social changes consequent upon industrial-capitalist-technological growth.[5]

If we think of the motor car again, we see that aspects of industrial production, such as specialization, uniformity, standardization, became common features of modern life. We assume that identical parts can replace worn or broken ones. What was true of the factory also became true successively of the department store, the farm and the office. F. W. Taylor gave his name to the system of intimately managed production, in which all tasks were broken down into their component parts, timed and checked in order to maximize productivity and profit. Henry Ford's assembly-line methods utilized carefully controlled management techniques to such extent that his name too was appropriated to sum up the approach: 'Fordism'. Each Model T that rolled out of Dearborn, Michigan, was inscribed with the marks of modernity. Such symbols, in turn, served to strengthen the system.

Differentiation

Marx may be the social analyst *par excellence* of early modernity – understood as capitalist society – but other sociologists also made distinctive contributions that help us grasp what was going on. The emerging industrial society was characterized by a steadily increasing division of labour, in which tasks became progressively more specialized. Emile Durkheim's (1858–1917) contribution was to suggest how this process of differentiation lay behind a new principle of social integration, what he called 'organic' rather than 'mechanical' solidarity. The latter, older type, relied on coercion and the heavy hand of tradition, whereas the former developed out of the growing interdependence fostered by the division of labour. An optimistic view, not shared by Marx, as we shall see.

Durkheim's sociology laid the groundwork for a major theme that would engage social scientists in the twentieth century: how differentiation spreads to all social spheres. Not only is 'work' split off from 'home' but also from 'leisure', 'religion' and so on. 'Public' life was by the same token distinguished from 'private' in novel ways, and along with these the lives of men and of women were also redefined in terms of specialist tasks. Among the middle classes, for instance, 'breadwinners' were distinguished from 'housewives' (this even where both partners were in paid employment). By the mid twentieth century, extended families would contract into nuclear, and become primarily units of consumption rather than production. Tasks once performed by the family or the Church were taken over by schools, youth cultures and the mass media on the one hand, or by local hospitals and welfare departments on the other.

During the twentieth century this theme would be taken up by Talcott Parsons and his school of sociology. Working on an organic analogy, Parsons suggested that new subsystems are constantly evolving, both differentiated from each other and better able to adapt, thus ensuring that as modernity progressed it would be better able to cope with its own problems. Differentiation would throw up problems of integration; in particular, how to coordinate complex society. The answer, for Parsons, lay in the creation of a meritocracy. Remove the old barriers to social involvement imposed by automatically ascribing people to particular roles and let them achieve what they can within a free market for skills and abilities. As Roland Robertson observes, Parsons's acceptance of modernity and his desire to find theoretical bases for its continued existence make Parsons a modern sociologist *par excellence*.[6]

Rationalization

Where Marx's sociology gives us a world of commodities, ruled by the restless pursuit of profit, and Durkheim's a world of detailed subdividing of tasks and responsibilities, Max Weber's (1864–1918) vision of modernity was somewhat different again. For him, rationalization is the key. By this he meant the gradual adoption of a calculating attitude towards more and more aspects of life. Having pushed what he saw as the 'spirits and demons' of traditional culture into the wings, the rational approach that underlay science and that found its most dynamic expression in the capitalist economy took centre stage, systematically infusing every sector of society. Authority derived more and more from this calculating rationality, less and less from tradition.

To observe, to calculate, these are the hallmarks of modernity for Weber. The scientist's laboratory method, the capitalist's ledger of profit and loss, the bureaucrat's rules and ranks within the organization, all testify to the significance of rationalization. Such careful calculation created control, it was a means to mastery. Nature could be 'tamed', cities rendered safe, workers made docile, books be balanced, and complexity contained, all by the application of the tool of rationality. The acme of efficient, productive organization, observed Weber, was the bureaucracy. But the same tendency spilled over into art and music as well; machine-like precision became a motif of painting, and music ran along lines of notation structured by new ideas of harmony. Whether for increasing crop yields, developing military precision, automating the household or coordinating airline schedules, rationalization became a central motif of modernity during the twentieth century.

Urbanism

A further sphere of rational organization was the city. Massive migration to mushrooming sites of industrial production, from the farms and villages of rural life, also spelled great social shifts. Although the precise definition of 'urban' has been a moot point – the United States became urban, it was said, when the majority of its population lived in settlements of 250 or more – it is clear that modern experience is overwhelmingly urban in contrast to a much more rural past. Georg Simmel, as we have seen, took the 'metropolis' to have a distinct effect on 'mental life', in addition to its being the centre of the money economy. As he said, 'Punctuality, calculability, exactness are forced upon life by the complexity and extension of metropolitan existence.'[7]

In many ways Simmel and others took the city to be the crucible in which modernity would be formed and reformed. Here in microcosm one would see differentiation, commodification and rationalization writ large. City dwellers were increasingly marked, he thought, by their blasé and reserved attitudes. They would give the appearance of, well, urbanity, thinking themselves the bearers of civilization, but distancing themselves from relationships that might be overly intimate. No longer would identity be found in the local community. The society of strangers had appeared, and it flourished in the city. A similar emphasis emerged in the work of Simmel's compatriot, Ferdinand Tönnies, who felt that modern life was marked more by formal and contractual relations than by those of *gemeinschaft*, community and communalism. Although this was also true in rural areas, it was accented in the urban.

Between the two world wars, the Chicago School of urban sociologists picked up this theme in powerful ways which would leave their stamp on much twentieth-century social analysis. For them, modernity was worked out in the burgeoning cities of the New World, above all in Chicago itself. Urbanism, they asserted, was nothing less than a new and distinctive 'way of life'. Here, the city became the means of processing the waves of immigrants, locating them in zones, and classifying them for use in the factories and offices of progressive industrialism. At the same time, the city retained an ambivalence, a feature to which we return in the next section.

Meanwhile back in the Old World, during the same inter-war

period, Le Corbusier was busy coming to terms with modernity in
the streets of Paris. Although nostalgia for pre-automobile days
marked his early thoughts on urbanism, he abandoned that for a
celebration of modernity. Reminiscent of Durkheim, this city
architect saw the potential of the very urban form for regener-
ation. New people needed a new type of street, that would be a
'machine for producing traffic'.[8] The city could be reconceptual-
ized from the vantage point of the car driver. No pedestrians or
sidewalk cafés would obstruct the flow of traffic. The city would
be built for cars. The elimination of the street would also eliminate crime and rebellion.

Discipline

Such a goal of modernity, rationally to exclude and eliminate the
criminal, the deviant, follows naturally from the classificatory, controlling impulse seen in sphere after sphere. The city was one such
sphere, but many others emerged. Modernity may also be related to
the rise of the military as a specialist aspect of the new nation state.
The uniform, the drill, the divisions into strict hierarchies of rank,
all were intended to make the military operate with efficiency and
to ensure that all fell into line. Military-style discipline was to have
a tremendous impact on the organizational patterns of industry,
administration and commerce, not to mention hospitals and
schools, in the modern era.[9]

Indeed, distinctive disciplinary tactics and strategies emerged
from the early modern period onwards. As sociological historians
from Max Weber to Michel Foucault and Norbert Elias have
shown, older ways of keeping order, such as the public and brutal
treatment of offenders, gave way to modes that emphasized self-
discipline, self-control. Such discipline came to characterize many
social contexts. Henry Ford's factories, for instance, turned out not
only motor cars but efficient workers, watched over by the infelic-
itously termed 'Sociology Department', that checked not only on
how well they worked on the shopfloor, but also on leisure-time
liquor and tobacco consumption![10] On the home front, Elias
demonstrates how the 'civilizing process' involved the refining of
table manners and the containment or concealing of sneezes or
passing wind.[11] Foucault, on the other hand, insists that in the
Panopticon prison plan we find the epitome of modern discipline.

Through a regime of unverifiable observation in which inmates are never sure when they are being watched, prisoners discipline themselves to keep order and to behave in keeping with the wishes of the prison administration. They end up, Foucault observes, as the 'bearers of their own surveillance'.[12]

Secularity

The Panopticon originated in the mind of Jeremy Bentham at the end of the eighteenth century. Mention of his name brings us to a final motif of modernity: the changing fortunes of religion. For Bentham's plan represented a self-conscious alternative to religiously rooted ways of dealing with offenders. Indeed, it was a secular parody of an all-seeing God. As the nineteenth century progressed, many examples appeared of alternatives to older religious forms, both deliberately fostered and as the unintended consequences of modernizing processes. Urban industrialism seemed to displace the influence of the churches in Europe both by displacing people from their older, communal contexts and by offering newer principles of social organization than those enshrined in religion. Eventually cityscapes would themselves display this process as steeples and church towers were dwarfed by commercial skyscrapers.

The French Revolution decisively dethroned God, proclaiming the arrival of the secular state. But as many, from Alexis de Tocqueville onwards, observed during the following century, this modern form was highly reminiscent of religion.[13] Admittedly, the horizon of hope had been lowered to this temporal life alone, but otherwise, elements of sacred doctrine, proselytism and even martyrdom all were there. Marx, Weber, Durkheim and Simmel each also noted in different ways the exchange of gods apparent in early modernity. Durkheim, for instance, believed that despite the apparently dismal outlook for Christianity, the essential forms of the religious life would persist in ways appropriate to the modern era. Simmel, on the other hand, did see new, mystical forms of religiosity coming into being, but felt that something vital was ebbing away.

Modernity, then, is a phenomenon of great diversity and richness, hard, if not impossible to summarize. Anthony Giddens, who has done more than most to encourage the use of 'modernity', sees it in terms of its major institutional areas. He helpfully suggests that it should be viewed, not as the outcome of some single overriding factor such as capitalism, but as a cluster of institutions. These include capitalism, industrialism, surveillance – seen especially in the nation state – and the military. All four of these are plainly evident in the foregoing account and, equally plainly, none can successfully be reduced to the others.

But at the same time something seems to be missing from this four-part scheme for understanding modernity. On the one hand, mention of raw materials and labour power for capitalist production reminds us that countries other than European ones were also involved in the project of modernity. Global interactions are far from new. Giddens neither ignores nor denies the importance of new ethnic relations, based in colonialism, but his original scheme has no obvious place for them. Likewise with gender. The Industrial Revolution wrought great changes in relations between the sexes, making women's special sphere domestic and men's public, thus reinforcing age-old patterns of dominance and subordination. Patriarchy took new, maybe more rigid forms within modernity.

The other near-absence from Giddens's scheme is culture, including the highly significant question of religion that resurfaces constantly.[14] Indeed, Giddens's rather rationalistic account seems almost impatient with the realm of feelings, the symbolic, and the spiritual. Yet the kaleidoscope of cultural colours is also in constant flux within modernity, and is chronically mixed up with the social shifts identified in Giddens's institutional approach. The ways that confident belief in progress eclipsed any trust in providence were manifest in architecture, art and rationalized social institutions. As we examine the ambivalence of modernity the cultural dimensions return to the foreground again and again, to be interwoven with the social, political and economic. So while the fourfold scheme of industrialism, capitalism, surveillance and military is very useful for encapsulating modernity, it also needs to be dovetailed with the dimensions of ethnicity and gender and of culture and religion.

Modernity's ambivalence

Modernity's achievement was to inaugurate nothing less than a new social order, to introduce unprecedented and often irreversible change on a massive scale. Indeed, modernity became the first mode of social organization to achieve global predominance. For many decades, the coming of modernity was viewed both by those who lived within it and those who aspired to it as offering overwhelming advantages over other ways of living. Who could refuse the pay packet, the Coke can and the phone? Little wonder trains, the telegraph, the telephone and television were seen as symbols of progress. The disruption caused to traditional cultures was viewed as little more than the temporary abrasion caused by transition to new circumstances. Class struggle, for instance, was to Durkheim not an endemic feature of capitalism, as it was for Marx, but the marker of a stage, preceding new forms of cooperation.

But modernity was a mixed blessing. From the earliest social analyses, notes of caution and concern were sounded. In the world of production Marx found exploiting capitalists and alienated workers. Durkheim noted a profound sense of unease, uncertainty about how to go on, among those affected by the new divisions of labour. Weber feared that rationalization would eventually crush the human spirit, walling it in behind the bars of the bureaucratic iron cage. Simmel sensed that the society of strangers would produce new social isolation and fragmentation.[15] And so on. By the later twentieth century, when reality caught up with these social scientific premonitions, modernity was seen as a mess. In fact, to many observers, things seemed worse than their forebears' fears. Perhaps modernity was creating the conditions for its own death.

Alienation and exploitation

Karl Marx, though he welcomed modernity, was no friend of its midwife, capitalism. The constant upgrading of technology, the dogged quest for market dominance, the increasingly global tentacles of capital, all these were aspects of a system designed to divide between those who profited and those who had nothing to lose but their chains. To Marx, capitalism succeeded in driving a wedge between capitalist and labourer, between labourers themselves – as they competed for scarce jobs – and, more profoundly, between workers and their own identity or 'species being'. Workers were thus both alienated from their own humanity, understood as free, purposeful activity, and exploited by an insatiable lust for profit. The real reward for their labour was always creamed off before the meagre wage was distributed.

Marx analysed capitalism as a total, integrated system, and his followers have tried to emulate him as capitalism has matured. Though many attempts have been made to discredit Marxism, most recently by associating its analytical stance with the ideology of state control under communism, many of its basic tenets retain their salience for today. While new phases of capitalism have undoubtedly emerged, such as Fordism from the First World War until after the Second, much evidence supports the Marxist claim that the restless drive towards capital accumulation continues unabated. The postmodern question is whether shifts in both the mode of production and in related regimes of regulation add up to a post-Marxist world or simply to more of the same, with a different name.[16]

Part of Marx's original project, though he did not know it, unleashed a whole genre of modernity critique. By observing that the money economy became the 'real community' he indicated that the world was becoming dominated by a system of impersonal, objective relations rather than the familiar, face-to-face ones of traditional societies. Our 'fetishism of commodities' hides from us the real nature of capitalist exchange and exploitation. It is impossible to discern, in that fragrant cup of coffee, the misery of the underpaid Brazilian bean-picker's family. Difficulties attend doing things at a distance. Others than Marxists have taken up the themes of superficiality, transitoriness, fractured relationships and obscured reality in modernity. But the Marxist distinctive is to see this violence, oppression and destructiveness as the direct result of capitalism itself.

Anomie and loss of direction

The sense of uprootedness from tradition, of having boundary markers disappear as it were overnight, appears strongly in the work of Durkheim. He saw a clear break occurring as modernity took hold. Traditional ties of family, kin and neighbourhood, torn by new mobility and lack of conventional regulation, were replaced only by a sense of uncertainty, loss of direction, and a feeling that the individuals were somehow on their own. Without some normative basis, a source of authority for society, thought Durkheim, the moral order would collapse. Whatever the eventual contribution of the organic solidarity of the division of labour, right now, argued Durkheim, this *anomie* was pathological, possibly to the point of suicide.

Succeeding developments, in which differentiation continued to divide social life into increasingly self-contained spheres, would probably have bothered Durkheim even more. The rules for each sphere – work, leisure, family, citizenship and so on – unlike the fairly unified rules and conventions of tradition, are developed within that sphere alone. Thus modern differentiation introduces decisively self-referential systems, which from an individual's perspective have constantly to be negotiated. Far from the single, overarching world of everyday life experienced in traditional societies, modernity brings a 'pluralization of lifeworlds'. The condition of anomie is reproduced again and again as, in Berger's telling phrase, 'homeless minds' accompany modernization.[17]

Durkheim's response to this, within his own sociological style, was to stress the scientific character of what he was doing. Who, after all, could return to religious themes like providence in an age of progress? Like his predecessor, Auguste Comte, he saw 'science' as superior to 'lay' knowledge, arguing that 'professional' judgements ought to be preferred above intuition and ordinary-life interpretations of reality. Science could in this way provide sure guidance in an age of anomie. Intellectuals had a clear role of leadership and legislation in the modern world. The corollary was the promise of 'rational' organization of society. Such a view remained popular and influential for many decades, to be openly – and rightly – challenged in the later twentieth century by both interpretive sociologies and by feminism.[18]

The iron cage

Plenty of gloomy prognoses were available regarding the future of modernity, but few were as relentlessly pessimistic as Max Weber's. None of Durkheim's upbeat prophecies of resolving modern dilemmas is echoed by Weber. Rather, he foresaw that the reign of rationality, applied equally in the social as in the natural environment, would produce the 'disenchantment of the world'. As 'substantive' was steadily ousted by 'formal' rationality, so any sense of the ultimate purposes of action would evaporate. Ironically, while modern liberal society was supposed to free people for involvement in more diverse ends, these actually faded into obscurity as people became enslaved to supposedly neutral techniques and technologies. Thus the ground was prepared for consumption itself to masquerade as an 'end'.

Weber reserved his most biting critique for modern rationality expressed in the bureaucracy. The bureaucratic official was for Weber the epitome of modernity. Bound by rules of rational procedure, untainted by 'irrational' considerations of race and religion, generation or gender, the bureaucrat was the indispensable functionary of commerce and industry, of capitalist enterprise and, prophesied Weber, the state socialist machine. In a world rapidly overrun by forces that stressed economic criteria alone, Weber feared that bureaucracy would simply hasten the inhumane. Not only would individuals suffer stunted development under its influence; democracy too was jeopardized by bureaucracy. In his own words:

> Together with the machine, the bureaucratic organization is engaged in building the bondage houses of the future, in which perhaps men will be like peasants in the ancient Egyptian State, acquiescent and powerless, while a purely technical good, that is rational, official administration and provision becomes the sole final value, which sovereignly decides the direction of their affairs.[19]

Weber was not alone in his anxiety about the rationalized world. Many writers and artists also expressed misgivings about the march of the machine and its accompanying social organization. The Victorian craftsperson and social critic William Morris, for instance, bemoaned the fragmentary nature of modern life and the dominance of economic values. He sought what he saw as genuine community based on a socialistic vision of revived medieval guilds. In the mid twentieth century the anti-rationalization cry would be taken up by critical theorists such as Theodor Adorno – 'the administered society' – or Herbert Marcuse – 'one-dimensional man' – and by the French sociologist Jacques Ellul in his devastating critique of a world reduced to 'technique' alone.[20]

'Bureaucracy, from the brutal to the banale' could be a book title for the twentieth century. For modernity in its bureaucratic mode has been discerned everywhere from Auschwitz to McDonalds. Writers such as Hannah Arendt and Zygmunt Bauman have shown how the Holocaust, so far from being an aberration from 'rational civilization', actually expressed it with exquisite cruelty. How else, than by considering Weber's dispassionate official, could we understand the concentration camp commandant who moved naturally between the gas chambers and his own children's playroom? At the banale extreme, George Ritzer suggests that the contemporary paradigm for formal rationalization is the fast-food restaurant.[21] Banale perhaps, but not trivial. If I am not mistaken, signs of McDonaldization – the quest for efficiency combined with obsession with the image – also seep subtly into the life of government departments, universities, sports clubs, churches and beyond.

The society of strangers

Perhaps it was because the city came to be seen as the crucible of modernity that ambivalence seems most marked there. While Weber's ultimate position on rationality is clear – it led not to the *philosophes'* dream of freedom but to the bureaucratic bondage of the iron cage – Simmel, and before him Charles Baudelaire, offered a much more nuanced view of urbanism. In 1863, Baudelaire, a French writer, published an essay on 'The Painter of Modern Life' which many now take to be one of the most prescient and insightful commentaries of the mid nineteenth century. Modernity, for Baudelaire, 'is the transient, the fleeting, the contingent; it is the one half of art, the other being the eternal and the immutable'.[22]

Baudelaire's famous figure, the *flâneur*, strolls through the streets and past the shops of the urban metropolis, thus gaining the truest view of quintessential modernity. Recognition of the fleeting, the transient, the superficial is the price to be paid for grasping what modernity is all about. The *flâneur* could get the best vantage point, said Simmel, precisely because he was anonymous, incognito. He was a stranger among strangers. The way to hold all this fragmentary experience together, according to both Baudelaire and Simmel, was through art. We still have to live as if there is something beyond the 'momentary reality' of modernity. Art is a way of making that elusive connection.

Art was not enough for Marx's colleague, Engels, however. He saw in the 'great city' of London the 'isolation of the individual – a narrow-minded egotism' that was nothing less than the 'disintegration of society into individuals, each guided by his private principles and each pursuing his own aims'.[23] And de Tocqueville, similarly ambiguous, saw Manchester as a 'foul drain' from which 'the greatest stream of human industry flows out to fertilize the whole world'.[24] This ambivalence about urban modernity persists as a theme well into the twentieth century, finding one of its landmark statements in Jane Jacobs's *The Death and Life of Great American Cities* (1961). She argued that while urban space was clean and orderly, it was socially and spiritually dead, except where life was sustained, paradoxically, by noise, congestion and chaos.

A further aspect of the cleanliness and order of many modern cities is seen in their treatment of 'others'. Since the 1960s especially, mobility and migration have vastly increased the ethnic and cultural variety of the world's great cities. This also means that larger and larger proportions of the population are difficult to classify. Neither friends nor enemies, these are both neighbours and strangers; unclassifiable others. As Madan Sarup says, 'Strangers often seem to be suspended in the empty space between a tradition which they have already left and the mode of life which stubbornly denies them right of entry.'[25] Such strangers tend to be stigmatized, as a reminder of their difference. At the same time, as Bryan Turner notes with reference to 'the Islamic question', 'The oil crisis, the Iranian revolution, the war in Afghanistan, the Gulf War and the global resurgence of Islamic fundamentalism' have made understanding these others a political necessity.[26]

Control

The ambivalence we have been discussing in relation to several social spheres resurfaces in the twin ideas of autonomy and control. For Max Weber and, later, for critical theorists, the Enlightenment promise of freedom as a product of rationality was a hollow one. Supposedly autonomous individuals, liberated from the authorities of tradition to forge their own destiny, find themselves mocked by the machine-like systems they now inhabit. According to Charles Taylor, it is just here that we see the three key 'malaises of modernity'.[27] Individualism, though it does emancipate us from given social orders, proceeds to confine us to 'the solitude of our own hearts' (de Tocqueville) and removes the heroic dimension of life, the purpose worth dying for. Then instrumental reason, that reduces everything to a level of cost–benefit analysis, represents further loss of autonomy. And the two are combined in the fear that 'soft despotism' will take over political power, bureaucratically organized, and unhindered by disinterested individuals busy seeking their own.

This motif of increased control may be seen at several levels. The regimes of power and discipline noted by Foucault with agencies such as social work or psychiatry represent one; and the apparently autonomous proliferation of new technologies and the technical fix outlook is another. Not for nothing does John Beniger see the history of the 'information society' as a 'control revolution'.[28] But this also spills over into the motif of mastery seen within modern patriarchy, where men assume systematic privileges and rights before women, and in the 'taming of nature' by technological means. The Canadian Ministry of Natural Resources sums up this attitude; seeing the created environment merely as a human 'resource'. Questions about the limits of such assumed human rights to 'use' nature have served only to deepen the sense of ambivalent modernity in the past few decades.

Unweaving the rainbow

Modernity's achievement, modernity's ambivalence: despite appearances, modernity has lived with inner doubts and contradictions from the start. And these are not just abstract or amorphous 'cultural' phenomena; they have been bound up with the messy materiality of money, machines, and streets. They inhere in the patterns and paths of social interaction. According to John Keats:

> Philosophy will clip an angel's wings,
> Conquer all mysteries by rule and line,
> Empty the haunted air, the gnomed mine –
> Unweave a rainbow.[29]

But as Weber reminds us, 'rule and line' could equally apply to bureaucratic memo and management, equally responsible for disenchanting the world. Not only magic and mystery but also authority and identity are dispelled or diffused by the coming of modernity.

Modernity has bequeathed to us a world split into social segments each governed by its own rules, implicit and explicit. Authority supposedly shifts from religious to scientific grounds, but in fact the main rule of thumb is instrumental, pragmatic: does it work? Is it efficient? The autonomous self moves to centre stage, claiming new liberties that will be enshrined in civil, political, social rights. But simultaneously that individual self loses a sense of meaning and purpose, a situation that has become a fundamental problem. As Giddens says:

The reflexive project of the self generates programmes of actualization and mastery. But as long as these possibilities are understood largely as a matter of the extension of the control systems of modernity to the self, they lack moral meaning. 'Authenticity' becomes both a preeminent value and a framework for self-actualization, but represents a morally stunted process.[30]

For many early moderns in the nineteenth century – especially those who were self-consciously so – religion could no longer offer a solution to this. The modern era seemed threatening to religion, and some felt, with Matthew Arnold, that the 'Sea of Faith . . . once, too, at the full' now left merely the sound of its 'melancholy, long, withdrawing roar'.[31] It was not just that deliberate efforts, like Bentham's, were made to secularize. Beyond this, the growth of a spirit of rational calculation, seen in science and capitalism, seemed to militate against miracle, faith and prayer. And the increasing involvement of the state in areas such as health and education once inspired and organized by the Church relegated the Church to a diminished role, so that public life was dominated more and more by principles alien to religion, leaving only a narrow margin of private life under the uncertain sway of religion. Or so the story went.

Modernity, it seemed to some, was digging its own grave. By proclaiming human autonomy, by setting in motion the process that would permit instrumental reason to be the rule of life, a change had begun which would end dismally, if not disastrously. Progress looked propitious, and was preferred over providence. But the promise of progress soured. Nothing would be immune from the dictates of sceptical, calculating reason, including reason itself. Yet ironically, many aspects of modernity seemed to spring from very religious sources; the Puritan emphases on careful observation of the work of God, on thrift and hard work had actually helped to stimulate early science and capitalism. Now, detraditionalization, secularization and rationalization were making a mockery of what seemed to be those honest, innocent beginnings.

How to deal with these contradictions, this unweaving, was seen quite differently by early moderns: Marx would overcome them; Weber despair of them; Simmel come to terms with them; and so on. As we shall see, a similar smorgasbord of solutions is offered by later moderns and postmoderns. The attitude to modernity is a crucial factor. Social theory is ever an amalgam of observable phenomena and contested commitments. By the later twentieth century, debate crystallized between those still wanting to come to terms with modernity and those seeing it as a terminus. Or, between those who admitted to a 'late' modernity and those who accepted *post*modernity. Paradoxically, the question was sharpened by a proposal that could be summed up as 'modernity reassured'. Daniel Bell, whose work is examined in the next chapter, called it 'postindustrialism'.

Modernity's incompleteness

One danger of considering modernity's achievements and ambivalence is that the concept may actually take on a life of its own, to be 'reified' into a self-propelling force that affects everything it touches. But it remains a mere concept, a mental construct, a grid for helping us organize our thinking about complex social realities. It helps to highlight certain features of contemporary life, such as the role of technology in facilitating new kinds of relationships. But, if taken to be a total system, it simply obscures as much as it illuminates. Later-twentieth-century social thought was obliged to grapple simultaneously with several aspects of modernity's incompleteness, with which the debate over postmodernity is closely bound up.

One defiant jolt comes from Bruno Latour, whose book title says it all: *We have Never Been Modern*. The confusion arises, he says, from two meanings of 'modern' – the time break distinguishing moderns from ancients, and the victory of the former over the latter.[32] Today, both the patent persistence of the premodern and the uncertainty about whether so-called revolutions express or expel old regimes lead to scepticism about the solidity of the modern achievement. But for Latour, that scepticism produces postmodern paralysis. It adds the insult of hyperreal weakness to the injury of invading technosciences, while not only (re)cutting ties with the past, but also breaking with the future. The biggest mistake of the postmoderns, charges Latour, is that they take moderns at their word, and assume that modernity is a seamless all-enveloping environment. It manifestly is not. The modern world never was 'disenchanted' in any more than a partial and limited fashion.

Recognizing that modernity, whatever it is, has not gone quite the way some of its original proponents intended has stimulated several kinds of analysis parallel to postmodern ones, but denying the logic of the latter. Alain Touraine speaks of a 'limited modernity', a period in which 'human beings mistook themselves for gods' but which ended with self-imprisonment within the despotism of totalitarian modernity.[33] The current crisis of modernity, for Touraine, represents not the denial of secularization and trust in reason, but a transition to a more complete modernity, in which Reason and the Subject will once more be affirmed. Without Reason, fears Touraine, the Subject is obsessed with identity; without the Subject, Reason becomes merely rationalizing power. Hope in humanity is reasserted and social movements are its bearer.

A similar stance is taken by Jürgen Habermas, for whom modernity is an unfinished project. It has yet to realize its full potential, and may do so, not through the social movements in which Touraine places his hopes, but through communicative action. Like Touraine, Habermas balks at the thought of instrumental reason riding roughshod through more and more spheres of life, but equally, he fears the rise of tribalisms and identity politics as the means of combating such reason's rule. The modern project may yet be carried forward by a theory of communication that can help mediate between different positions. Against the universalism that denies and crushes particularity, he posits, not a postmodern penchant for particularity that denies universals, but a search for means to mutual understanding and a listening that respects the other. The quest is a worthy one, and theoretically suggestive, but it certainly seems to take us a long way beyond empirical sociology.

Habermas's German compatriot, Ulrich Beck, takes another tack, one that is grounded much more firmly in the conflicts and fears of daily life. For Beck, the real problem is risk.[34] The modern project is chronically incomplete, says Beck, because of the unacknowledged effects of its central dynamic. Whereas once the single-minded drive towards wealth production was pursued with impunity, the resulting risk production now confronts us with the question of how to contain, prevent, minimize, or limit the damage caused by the relentless process of production. The question is pushed deeper by the unfortunate facts that today's dangers are often scarcely perceptible (for example, health hazards near industrial plants; growing rents in the ozone layer), have to be calculated as probabilities, and yet are all too often privatized, thus deflecting attention from their true causes. Beck thus exposes a dark side of modernity and argues that risk management has now become one of its central features. Technoscientific knowledge is invoked to counter risks, but, as Beck stresses, risk discourses also inevitably involve ethical stances, which implies a moral economy of knowledge production.[35]

The self-consciousness of risk society that constantly monitors mercury levels in water or calculates the chances of epidemics and industrial accidents, is highlighted in Anthony Giddens's concept of 'reflexive' modernity. Modernity as the application of technoscience to industrial production meets its nemesis in oil spills, smogs, dustbowls and meltdowns. But widespread awareness of this, individually and institutionally, remakes modernity without rejecting it. Giddens gets the prize for producing prefixes to modernity, having come up with 'late', 'high', and 'radicalized' as well as 'reflexive' modernity.[36] As he understands it, *high* modernity accentuates certain features of modernity, especially the influence of distant happenings on local events, and on the self, mediated by electronic modes of communication. Despite the fact that these are just the social indicators that persuade others to speak of *post*-modernity, Giddens maintains that good reasons exist for not going there. Yet.

From Postindustrialism to Postmodernity

'Staccato signals of constant information . . .'
Paul Simon, 'Boy in a bubble'

Sociologists specialize, it seems, in announcing the arrival of new kinds of society. Sometimes this is little more than hype, and scepticism is in order. But in sociology's early twentieth-century classical period, it was just such ambitious announcements that gave the discipline a sense of social relevance if not public credibility. The need to find an angle from which to observe processes and relationships undergoing radical upheaval, resulting in novel configurations of the social landscape, stimulated the sociological imagination and challenged the conceptual frameworks which hitherto had served to express social realities.

Something similar is happening today. In the later part of the twentieth century it was the turn of 'orthodox' sociology to be questioned as a set of taken-for-granted verities. Too many features of the social world appeared to be changing simultaneously for the new situation to be seen simply as an extension of modernity. Today we are confronted by a plethora of new names for these transformations – the risk society, the global age, the information society, postindustrialism, the communicative era, the second media age; plus those that simply add a prefix to what has gone before, producing late modernity, high modernity, meta-modernity, hyper-modernity, super-modernity, and, of course, postmodernity.

It is worth noting the origins of social forecasts that began in the 1960s. At this time the first serious hints that a 'new kind of society' was in the making came from Daniel Bell. Though others had used the term before him, he popularized the notion of postindustrialism. Forget the 'factory worker' image of industrialism; the new professional and technical 'elite' of the service sector had become pre-eminent.[1] The fresh phase of industrial society was based above all on theoretical knowledge. Industrialism would be transformed by the use of new information and communication technologies, which would do for mental power what machines, in the industrial revolution, had done for muscle power. Bell later said that the new condition would be an 'information society'.

As far as modernity is concerned, the information society could be thought of as 'modernity renewed', given a new lease of life. Progress is still possible, if we cling to Enlightenment claims about reason, now digitally encoded. However, some of the social and technical conditions Bell called postindustrialism actually helped prepare the ground for what is typical of the postmodern. Here again, the social and the cultural may be seen to act upon each other. Pluralism and perspectivism, uncertainty and mental homelessness, are not hindered by the tilt (exaggerated by Bell) towards service jobs, computers and TV. Just the contrary.

Bell himself was not blind to this possibility. Indeed, he perceived certain 'cultural contradictions of capitalism' in which the Apollonian principle of regulation engaged in dramatic struggle with the Dionysian principle of energy, sexuality and experience.[2] But these contradictions were only indirectly connected with the new technologies of information and communication. Rationality would be called in question and a new hedonism would flower, he suggested. In the quest for new forms of legitimation and a new social bond to replace both those of tradition and of modernity, Bell wondered whether a 'return to the sacred' might become evident. In the late 1970s Lyotard, who took up much of Bell's postindustrial thesis, had no such thoughts, however.

Paradoxically, where Bell's postindustrialism still rests on an implicit concept of progress, others such as Lyotard anticipate postindustrialism without progress. The consequences of the new technologies, seen in new kinds of flexible production, in media-centredness and in the rapid rise of contemporary consumerism, are still present. But in postmodern accounts these now frame reality; no forward movement, no ultimate improvement is envisaged. The question is, does dependence upon these new technologies really

take us beyond modernity? Are cybernetics and surveillance har-
bingers of an immaterial, postmodern world of virtual realities and
dispersed selves? Is the Babel of communicative society, where
varied voices vie for attention, our inevitable and desirable condition, or is this communicative interference and distortion to be
overcome?

Postindustrialism and information society: the modern story

Proponents of postindustrialism, as the word suggests, proposed
that the 'advanced' societies were moving beyond an historical era
that could be described as 'industrial'. A fundamental shift was
occurring, such that the very 'axial principles' of society were
increasingly located in 'theoretical knowledge' as opposed to 'capital and labour'. Just as agrarian societies based on the land had
given way to industrial, based on manufacturing, so new service-
based societies were coming into being. Daniel Bell's postindustrial
society provided the 'social framework' for the 'information
society' in which telecommunications and computers would
become 'decisive for the way economic and social exchanges are
conducted, the way knowledge is created and retrieved, and the
character of work and organizations in which men [sic] are
engaged'.[3]

This postindustrial, or, as its shape supposedly became clearer,
information society[4] theme was taken up by many researchers and
policy-makers, in a number of different countries.[5] Though some,
such as observers in France and Japan, assumed that government
initiatives would be vital to its success, while others, in countries
such as the UK and the USA, decided to let market forces lead the
way, there was considerable convergence in eventual outcomes.
Two reports in the early and mid-1980s, for instance, enjoined
Canadians to be *Planning Now for an Information Society* and discussed the *Uneasy Eighties* as a 'transition to an information
society'.[6] Grounded in the assumption that microelectronics-based
technologies portended a 'quantum leap in human capabilities',
these reports worked with the notion that an 'information
economy' was emerging, citing the rise in proportion of infor-
mation-related occupations from 21 per cent to 40 per cent between
1931 and 1971.[7] In a fairly upbeat manner it was suggested that,

with the political will plus appropriate investment and sound educational policies, the transition to the information society was a feasible next stage of development. Warnings were also mentioned regarding competition from Europe and the Third World, and about negative consequences such as unemployment and loss of personal autonomy.

Such arguments continued into the 1990s. One claims that today in Canada 'the information society is now as clearly visible as the postindustrial society'.[8] Dependent on the new 'information [technology] environment' this change involves 'a new way of thinking and acting' because technology is now an 'integral part of culture'.[9] Others consider Canada as an information society on a number of interrelated criteria.[10] If one examines international trade in information technology (IT) products, then Canada, though only a minor player in global IT export terms, saw the IT sector of the GDP rise from 5.5 per cent in 1990 to 7.6 per cent in 1995.[11] Per capita telephone concentration is among the highest in the world, having risen from 21 per 100 in 1950 to 63 per 100 in 1985. By 1995, 98.5 per cent of Canadian households had telephones, 73.4 per cent had cable television, 28.8 per cent owned computers and 12.1 per cent owned modems.[12]

The service sector, strikingly, had grown from 47.3 per cent in 1956 to almost 70 per cent by 1987. The proportion of women in the labour force and the burgeoning of environmental concern are viewed as further indicators relating to the Canadian information society. Stern warnings are issued in Canada that if the 'penurious' level of spending on research and development (R&D) continues – hovering between 1.1 per cent and 1.4 per cent of GDP in the mid-1980s, and up only to 1.5 per cent by 1991,[13] which is half that of the USA, Japan, Germany and the UK – then Canada's information society status could again be 'vulnerable'. Progress must not be thwarted.

These accounts betray their reliance on a common core of theorizing about postindustrialism and information society that can best be traced to Bell. Above all is the assumption of fundamental discontinuity with 'industrial society' as services become the dominant economic sector and as theoretical knowledge (seen especially in terms of R&D) becomes the axial principle. But these assumptions have increasingly been questioned. Rising employment in the service sector has been a feature of industrial societies since their inception, argues one, and in any case, 'services' is a pretty vague ragbag of occupations, says another.[14] Similarly, with regard to R&D, this has been a basic feature constitutive of industrial society. What may be more significant are the features omitted from the popular accounts, such as the heavy and persistent dependence on the military sector for R&D.[15] Information and communication technologies are not just an innocent 'given', as some information society accounts imply.[16]

Several other features deserve mention, and I shall highlight two. First, an impression was given – and still persists in some accounts – that the information society is one in which the benefits of new technology will be distributed in a roughly equitable fashion. For instance, while new technology-related unemployment is a matter for ongoing controversy, it is less than prominent in the work of Bell and those who follow in his steps. As a social reality, however, high levels of unemployment persist in an era of technological and economic restructuring, despite apparent growth. Productivity growth no longer spells job creation, it seems. It is also the case that work has become much more flexible: many jobs are being casualized, women enter the labour force but at a disadvantage to men, and so on. The concepts of full employment, lifelong careers and job security, are largely a memory. Translate such statistics into human costs, and the cultural consequences of economic change become clearer. Uncertainty and risk come to characterize both social and cultural spheres.

Moreover, that uneven advantage is geographically accented. Certain depressed areas, such as the Canadian Maritimes, suffer unemployment levels around 20 per cent, whereas the invidiously nicknamed 'sunrise' areas, such as Vancouver, have much lower levels than the national average. This does not mean, of course, that the centre of economic power is moving westwards in Canada. As Harold Innis observed in the 1950s, centre–periphery relations within the massive geography of Canada have been established since the beginning of settlement in favour of the east-central metropolitan areas around Toronto and Montreal. However much the potential of new technology may point to the possibilities for novel sites for 'informational' expansion[17] the reality is that traditional centres of manufacture and innovation tend still to offer benefits such as an existing financial, labour and transport infrastructure.[18]

This kind of continuity is also strong in Europe, where a crescent-shaped series of such centres of innovation, from London, England, through an eastern arc to Torino, Italy, has been in evidence since the fiftecnth century, when printing and humanistic learning were its main features. Nor is this continuity mitigated by the development of those 'high-tech fantasies', science and technology parks, supposedly modelled on Silicon Valley, California. As Doreen Massey and others say, with particular but not exclusive reference to Britain, science parks are elitist experiments that serve to increase social polarization and geographical inequality.[19] Even Silicon Valley exhibits this, with its contrasting concentrations of low-skill labour in San Jose and high-skill, high-tech in Los Altos or Cupertino. In Canada, while demand remains fairly high for a limited number of university-qualified people in areas such as health care or software design, located in Montreal or Vancouver, job opportunities are shrinking in just those fields that used to offer a chance to the low-skilled, such as fish canning and textile factories.[20] And beyond the affluent world of the North Atlantic, of course, such geographical disparities are seen on a global scale. All too often, the 'information age' in underdeveloped countries spells a struggle for basic literacy. As Zygmunt Bauman notes, 'a particular cause for worry is the progressive breakdown of communication between the increasingly global and extraterritorial elites and the evermore "localized" rest'.[21]

The information age also means greater flexibility in management, with the concomitant expectation of flexible employment. Financial markets are globalized, with crucial manufacturing and location decisions being taken more and more remotely from where their effects are felt on the ground. More networking of companies exists, along with more individualized and diverse forms of employment. Labour unions have been disempowered, welfare states dismantled, and competitive market forces unleashed in more and more sectors of social and political life. Whereas once the worker was seen as an irrational element in the predictable economic machine, now the machine itself seems unpredictable. You never know when some big company will gobble up a smaller one, or when a production plant will close down, only to be reopened elsewhere. No 'certainties' are available any more; the world of 'freedom of choice' seems also to be a world of unprecedented risks.

Another less-discussed feature of the so-called information society is the role of information technology in control and surveillance. In everyday life, most mundane relationships are mediated by computer, whether via bankcards, healthcards, credit cards, phonecards, driving licences, storecards, workplace access cards or whatever. These technologies express a demand for greater coordination and control of technical and social processes, the latter relating to citizens, employees and consumers. While much is made of the potential for decentralization using new technologies, there seems to be a simultaneous shift to greater centralization of some operations. Even decentralization is compatible with increasing overall control, although no particular agency may be behind it.[22] The need for such surveillance is created by the risks of an individualized, private, uncertain world, where more and more is done at a distance. Companies and governments seek tokens of trustworthiness before they can grant privileges, benefits and services. But paradoxically, that search for trust is construed in turn as a threat to privacy, or even freedom.

Administrative databases contain increasing amounts of personal data, gleaned from systems employed by the police, health care, taxation, welfare and unemployment benefits, immigration, driver and vehicle licensing, education and so on. *De facto* national databases emerge as extensive computer matching makes profiling of individuals increasingly easy. Such profiles may also be built commercially, and often on a much larger scale, through the use of matching routines between credit companies and organizations that specialize in collating personal data on consumption and lifestyle.[23] This phenomenon grows faster than government surveillance. Locally, Compusearch Market and Social Research, for example, garners data from Statistics Canada and overlays them with data from Canada's 650,000 postal codes to create detailed sociodemographic portraits as an aid to niche marketing strategies.[24] Not only would they manufacture our needs but also channel our desires. This virtual world has huge implications for life chances and for (post)modern politics.[25]

Other questions should also be raised about postindustrialism. Prominent among these are the assumption that the USA would lead the way into the information age, and the neglect of gender within the analysis of postindustrialism. It has become clear over recent years that Japan has a strong claim to leadership, not only in technological innovation, but also in its attempts to balance that with other aspects of manufacturing and social-cultural life. Pacific rim countries – especially the 'Asian tigers' of Japan, Korea, Taiwan and Singapore – must now all be counted as playing crucial roles in postindustrial developments. And it is hard to imagine how any worthwhile analysis can proceed without paying close attention to the massive growth of female participation in the labour force of the advanced societies, with its consequences in all social spheres.

Today, much more uncertainty than was evident a decade ago attends discussions of the 'impact' of information technology. Even the author of one of the above-mentioned Canadian reports now speaks in more sober tones about the 'perils of an information age'. In particular he has in mind our apparent inability to 'integrate new information into a meaningful context'.[26] Another commentator whose work on 'high-tech society' has become increasingly critical is Tom Forester. He argues that 'all talk of . . . "megatrends" and "postindustrial" societies must now be taken with a large pinch of salt'.[27] He highlights the failure of predictions regarding automated factories, paperless offices, electronic cottages, and so on, as examples of exaggerated technical claims and marketing dreams, and comments on the unintended consequences of greater security and surveillance risks, vulnerability of technology dependence and computer crime. He concludes with a plea for rehumanization of technology development.

The modern story of postindustrialism and information society is one suffused above all with the belief in progress. The social and the cultural are mutually supporting. Improvement and development through the application of new technologies is assumed. Many still believe that eventually all parts of the world will benefit from this technological revolution, a cruel neo-colonial self-deception if ever there was one. The core ideas of the modern story persist in various futuristic publications – such as Nicholas Negroponte's *Being Digital* or Bill Gates's *The Road Ahead* – but also in the work of social scientists who propagate theories such as those emanating from Kondratieff's 'carrier waves' of technology and economic development.[28] Characteristic of these is the downplaying of social and geographical polarization – even the concept of the 'information poor' has an ironic and insulting ring when chronic starvation confronts millions on a daily basis – and the risks associated with IT diffusion.[29] Meanwhile the literature that now questions the earlier optimism concerning information society exudes a sense of disappointed dreams, that progress has somehow slowed, stumbled or stopped.

Postindustrialism and the end of progress: the postmodern story

Though his starting point is similar, building on the postindustrial ideas of Bell but also of Alain Touraine, Lyotard's *The Postmodern Condition* (1979) paints a picture of a world beyond progress. 'It is hard', he observes, 'to see what other direction contemporary technology could take as an alternative to the computerization of society.' In this situation, Lyotard's central point is that the 'status of knowledge is changing'. But his complaint about the idea of the 'computerization of society' is that 'it fails to challenge the general paradigm of progress in science and technology, to which economic growth and the expansion of socio-political power seem to be natural complements'.[30] The metanarrative of progress can no longer be assumed.

Whereas Bell distinguishes between economy, polity and culture, seeing science and technology as the motor of social change, in contrast with the 'narcissism' of contemporary 'culture', Lyotard discusses science itself as a 'form of discourse' whose aleatory character is limited or local. Bell views science (as an aspect of the new 'axial principle') as more than mere discourse; it is disinterested, as in Robert Merton's classic account, and refers clearly to external reality. Lyotard, however, reconnects science with culture, noting that the commercialization of research means that we are dealing not so much with the discovery of truth as the augmentation of power.[31] There is no guarantee that Reason produces liberating consequences.

Education itself, which under the sway of Enlightenment thought came to be seen either as a moment in the progressive unfolding of freedom, as in France, or as a means of promoting national health, as in Germany, is now reduced to performativity, to training and skills. In Lyotard's view, the advanced societies are increasingly bound up with finding 'the optimal contribution of higher education to the best performativity of the social system'.[32] Thus emancipatory reason gives way to technocratic rationalization. As Robins and Webster say in their blistering critique of *The Technical Fix*, 'when the systematic production of operational skills and competences has become the objective of the socio-technical system, then appeal to emancipatory truths and values can be seen to be out of its time'.[33]

New technology retains a significant place within Lyotard's analysis. He insists that 'along with the hegemony of computers comes a certain logic, and therefore a set of prescriptions determining which statements are accepted as "knowledge" statements'.[34] Knowledge is not sought for its own sake, but is legitimated by 'performativity' and becomes increasingly commodified. So for Lyotard, power and its self-legitimation have everything to do with data storage and accessibility. In various contexts, control is enhanced by the 'computerization of society'.[35] As he says:

> By reinforcing technology, one 'reinforces' reality and one's chances of being just and right increase accordingly. Reciprocally, technology is reinforced all the more effectively if one has access to scientific knowledge and decision-making authority.[36]

More generally, we hear the echo of contemporary managerialism in this account. Increasingly, within a market-led world, managerial solutions are sought to contemporary dilemmas. This is true not only of the proper stewarding of companies, but also in that governments are now expected to manage the economy, and management is the keyword in the health services and even in corrections and the treatment of offenders. Where legislative reason once reigned, and professionals at least paid lip-service to codes of ethics relating to the matter in hand – preservation of life, punishment for law-breaking – now the common language of management takes over, apparently regardless of the specificity of the social sphere in which it operates. 'Information management' is simply the latest development within this trend.

Information technology plays a double role in Lyotard's account. On the one hand it fosters the postmodern condition by promoting cybernetics as a novel language game. On the other, IT expresses some key motifs of modernity, extending performativity like a prosthetic aid. Control is maximized even as ambivalence and contingency are minimized. However, it must be said that Lyotard's stress is on the splitting of modernity into language games, the dissolution of philosophical hierarchy. He has precious little to say about the kind of political economy that concerns Bell, assuming that the social can be atomized (away) into languages games. By this move

Lyotard misses the chance of exploring some deep underlying shifts, such as the partial freeing of politics and ideas from the yoke of the economy, which might have given his work a more socio-logical resonance. As it is, Lyotard largely sidesteps the question of *social* transformation to which his concept of the postmodern seems to refer.

That question has been taken up by many others, however, par-ticularly those working within more empirical traditions.[37] Discus-sions of 'post-Fordism' have now become part and parcel of the debate over postmodernity. Starting with Ford, it is noted that the five-dollar, eight-hour day at his assembly lines was intended both to ensure worker compliance with the regime of industrial produc-tion and to line the workers' pockets with enough to take advan-tage of the consumer products being churned out. By the 1970s, however, falling demand for standardized, mass-produced goods, plus competition from newly industrialized countries such as those on the Pacific rim, stimulated the search for new production tech-niques, less rigid and confining than Fordism. Flexible manufacture – post-Fordism – introduced a more volatile labour market, faster switches from one product or style to another, and a far greater con-sumer orientation. A scramble for new technologies, new patterns of management and new global interconnections, from finance capital to markets, was the result.

What we have in Lyotard, then, is a theory of postmodernity quite different from the 'postindustrial' or 'information' society theories with which we began. Indeed, the very processes under discussion seem to deflect attention from discrete 'societies' to postmodernity as a *global* condition. Nonetheless they touch on many of the same symptoms, transmuted as the phenomena of postmodernity. Lyotard's account leaves us in a philosophical and linguistic mael-strom, although some of his comments on the consequences of the new technologies are suggestive. The post-Fordism thesis, on the other hand, reminds us of concrete changes in the industrial and consumption landscapes, changes that are crucial for understanding the significance of communication and of consumerism within theories of postmodernity.

New technology and society: beyond modernity?

As Barry Smart observes, interest in postmodernity 'seems to have displaced the former preoccupation with the prospect of a transition to postindustrial society at the centre of intellectual debate in the West'.[38] The question is, why? Smart's answer is salient: western civilization itself seems to be undergoing irreversible transformation at an accelerating pace, and can no longer sustain the belief that it is a 'paradigm for "progress"'. This does not imply that technology is insignificant. For Lyotard and others, technological transformations are profoundly implicated in the conditions they now describe.[39] A variety of postindustrial theory has somehow survived its earlier critical battering to be recycled as postmodernity.

The relative paucity of technological content in many theories of postmodernity is striking. Yet the issues raised by both debates are important. Modern theories of social and cultural life are being burst apart by new structures of time and space that are directly associated with the global development of information and communication technologies. The failure to integrate the social aspects of new technologies in new sociologies of postmodernity can only be detrimental to our grasp of what is going on today. At the same time, the belief, often undergirding older social theories, that technological advancement necessarily promotes the progress of human civilization is false, as the history of the twentieth century (and not just the monumentally symbolic failures of Titanic, Bhopal, or Challenger) attests so forcefully. But to abandon progress need not also entail forsaking commitments either to understanding or to guiding technological development.

One theorist who tries to retain a 'critical' edge to theories of postmodernity is Mark Poster. He proposes that a 'mode of information'[40] is supplanting previous sociocultural formations, and his comments pick up on the twin themes arising from Lyotard's work mentioned above: control *and* contingency. Poster argues that 'the solid institutional routines that have characterized modern society for some two hundred years are being shaken by the earthquake of electronically mediated communication and recomposed into new routines whose outlines are as yet by no means clear'.[41] He focuses on TV-based media, the surveillance capacities of information technology, electronic writing and computer science, proposing that action-based social theory – typical of modernity – is no longer appropriate for understanding them. To follow through on Lyotard's emphases, though, Poster comments on both the peculiarity of computer science as a language game, and on the extension of power using IT.

Computer science, it has been observed, must be the only

discipline founded on a machine, a situation that brings interesting consequences, not least of which is the inability to know when computer scientists have become subjects of the instruments they created to be their subjects. An early expression of this in film was Hal, in *2001 A Space Odyssey*, or the even more sinister cyborg in *Terminator*, that tried to ensure the final tyranny of the machine. The process flagged by Lyotard, in which knowledge legitimated by computers passes as the 'real', may be less visually dramatic but no less challenging for conventional theories of knowledge. It becomes visible in artificial intelligence: 'The scientist projects intelligent subjectivity onto the computer and the computer then becomes the criterion by which to define intelligence.'[42] Cognate studies have shown how computer-generated data is often taken more seriously than other data, which also supports Lyotard's position.

As for IT extending social power prosthetically, Poster engages at length with the question of databases, this time using Foucault as a foil. Poster views electronic surveillance as a 'superpanopticon' that not only strengthens the power of 'knowledge' but also reconstitutes and multiplies the 'selves' that are its object.[43] Like Lyotard, he comments particularly on the commodification of this information, connecting it with consumerism. He also sees elements of social control expanding in this situation, control that is in some ways more insidious to the extent that it is little understood. But it is control that needs no external justification, based as it is on ongoing knowledge of simulated situations.[44] Its influence seems to increase, even as the visible workings of its machinery become more opaque.

While it is clear that Poster sees in the new technologies great potential for new forms of domination, less clear is what modes of resistance might be appropriate. He accepts that Lyotard's proposed strategy – 'give the public free access to the memory and databanks' – might be one way forward, but does not appear to have a lot of confidence in this tactic.[45] The reason is that the mode of information contains within itself 'disintegrating impulses' which might render any kind of 'communal' action inappropriate. Among other things, identities tend to be fractured in cyberspace, which renders questionable any simple comparisons between on-line and off-line sociality.[46] While electronically mediated communication does in some ways supplement existing modes of communication, it also shows signs of substituting for them in ways that we do not yet understand. In other words, these new technologies help to propel us into unknown social terrain, that of postmodernity.

The question of electronically mediated communication is central to postmodern debates. Although he has suffered a similar fate to Bell – his work is often dismissed as flawed and *passé* – in the 1960s Marshall McLuhan captured some of the sense in which electronic media have become crucial to understanding the late twentieth century. While some hype certainly resides in the notion of a 'global village', the idea does highlight some important effects of the new media. Distant events are instantly available, in glorious or gory technicolour (to people with the right equipment), across the globe. Moreover they affect our responses to relationships and to crises such as death. By telephone, connected through satellites, we may talk in real time using our voices, or converse by electronic mail, with friends or colleagues thousands of kilometres away.

It is a commonplace of sociological descriptions of modernity that our relationships have been stretched in unprecedented ways across time and space. For earlier generations, the development of writing made mediated relationships possible on a wide scale, and printing extended this further. But the process has accelerated during the twentieth century as first the telegraph, then phones, radio, TV and now computers and telecommunications have appeared in rapid succession, facilitating everything from live global coverage of events like the Super Bowl to the constant circulation of capital around the world in a never-closing stock exchange. Where once many little 'worlds' existed, now there is but one. A TV documentary in the United Kingdom filmed World Cup night soccer fans in Australia, Finland, Iran, Italy and Nigeria, showing that their preparations for the game, and their responses to each goal scored, were almost identical in each country! When writing the first edition of this book, I had just received a letter from my daughter, working on a community project in Honduras. She spoke of the beauties of the rainforest and of visiting a Pizza Hut in Tegucigalpa – both now vivid and poignantly contrasting symbols of 'one world'.

But postmodern accounts of communication technologies frequently focus on the converse of global unity, new kinds of dispersal and fragmentation. For Baudrillard, the new electronic media presage a world of pure simulacra, of models, codes and digitality, of media images that have become the 'real', or rather, that erode any distinction between the 'real' world and that of the pervasive media. Indeed, one casualty of this may be society itself, or 'the social' as Baudrillard put it. 'Mass media' may turn out to be a misnomer, as the effect of the media is to show how the social itself was an illusion, and along with it traditional political strategies.[47]

The idea that reality is being broken down into images is common within postmodern discourse. Life is being dissolved into TV in Baudrillard's hyperreal world. While some take this to mean that codes multiply, Baudrillard also sees this process as unifying, or at least leading to homogeneity; hyperreality is likened to a genetic code. However, it is hard to see how a world of TV advertising images would be anything but fragmented, except in the sense that those images all originate in a consumer capitalist context. The question of homogeneity and heterogeneity persists in the debates over globalization.

Giddens makes two criticisms of Baudrillard's world of 'hyperreality'. He argues that the pervasive and constitutive role of electronic media in our social relationships in Baudrillard's account is confused with the self-referential character of modern social institutions. The fact that modern media may help to form, as well as to mirror, realities does not add up to a situation in which sign or image is everything. And when media presentations juxtapose stories and items that have no obvious logical or meaningful connections, the resulting 'collage' should not necessarily be taken to mean the demise of narrative, or the severance of signs from their referents. Rather, suggests Giddens, 'the separate stories which are displayed alongside one another express orderings of consequentiality typical of a transformed time-space environment from which the hold of place has largely evaporated'.[48]

Beyond this, one might add that the knowledgeability of TV watchers should not be underplayed. How audiences decode TV in their living rooms is an issue in its own right.[49] Soccer fans in different countries might watch games similarly, but even this does not mean that they have been reduced to stimulus–response machines. Television audiences, and consumers in general, are often skilful and creative users of communications media. As Featherstone observes, 'Television and the new communications technology are frequently presented as producing both manipulation and resistance, and the homogenization and fragmentation of contemporary culture.'[50]

But if Baudrillard's hyperreal world of communication may be overstated, this still leaves untouched other aspects of contemporary communication that are important for the postmodern debate. Gianni Vattimo, for instance, sees contemporary society as characterized primarily by 'generalized communication'. It is 'the society of the mass media'.[51] The passing of modernity occurs, in his view, when history can no longer be seen as unilinear; it is just the past from a series of different viewpoints. The demise of history drags progress down with it as well. While Vattimo's 'transparent society' is in part the result of collapsed colonialism and imperialism, which make it clear that the European way is not the only one, it is even more the creation of mass communication.

Against Theodor Adorno, the critical theorist who once predicted the homogenization of society through the mass media, Vattimo insists that 'radio, television and newspapers became the elements in a general explosion and proliferation of *Weltanshauungen*, of world views'.[52] So, far from Orwell's Big Brother dominating everyone, all sorts of minorities now take to the microphones. The continuous expansion of communications produces what Vattimo sees as 'apparently irresistible pluralization'. Thus Nietzsche's 'true world becoming a fable' is seen in the ways that our understanding of reality is composed of multiple 'images, interpretations and reconstructions circulated by the media in competition with each other and without any "central" coordination'.[53]

For Vattimo, emancipation lies right here. Not in the perfect knowledge of one who knows how things really are, which was the secularized 'God's-eye view' view of the Enlightenment, followed by Hegel or Marx, but freedom within plurality, the erosion of the reality principle itself. Is this erosion such a big loss after all, he asks? We exchange the world of objects, measured by techno-science, for the world of merchandise and images, the phantasmagoria of the mass media. Nostalgia for past stable, authoritative realities could end as neurosis. Rather, liberty should be sought in *disorientation*. Not the discovery of who we 'really' are as blacks, women and so on, but just the discovery of the finitude, historicity and contingency of our own identities and value systems.

Rather more analytically, Roland Robertson ties the question of reality to processes of globalization. This links directly, of course, with the growth of communications, on which globalization depends. Robertson also sees nostalgia creeping back as reality is

challenged, nostalgia for the global order of 1880–1925, which was
the occasion for hot and cold war until the 1980s. National societies
confront both problems of diversity and pressure to be pluralistic.
Individuals are subject to competing ethnic, cultural and religious
reference points; international relations is becoming more multi-
polar; and even any fixed sense of 'humanity' cannot be assumed
any more.[54] The concept of globalization is indeed inextricably
bound up with the debate over the postmodern.

The global and the postmodern

Is globalization an outcome of the logic of modernity, such that
'modern' effects will ripple out into more and more contexts, cour-
tesy of the new technologies? Or does globalization represent a
new era, beyond modernity, which will require the overhaul of all
modern social theories? Either way, how does the global situation
relate to the postmodern? If globalization is a consequence of
modernity, then presumably it will foster further modern social and
cultural processes, and the postmodern need not enter the picture.
But if globalization helps propel societies beyond the modern, then
the concept is either a competitor with, or a complement to, postmodernity.

When globalization is viewed as a consequence of modernity
there is a tendency to see capitalist developments continuing in a
fairly linear fashion, producing uniform and standardized results,
such as McDonaldization. The western way tends to predominate,
for better or worse, with the result that uniformity becomes more
universal. The spread of English as an official or a technical language, or the renewed exporting of the American way of life would
be evidence of such a trend. Greater social, economic, political and
cultural homogeneity would be the outcome.

While this is not far removed from the old orthodoxy of mid-
century 'modernization' theory, propounded by W. W. Rostow,
even modernization's best known critic, the 'world systems' theorist Immanuel Wallerstein, sees globalization and modernity as
being of a piece.[55] For the latter, however, the crucial move was to
see the basic unit of analysis not as a 'nation state' or a 'society' but
as a social 'totality'. On this account, only world empires, world
economies or autonomous subsistence economies qualify as units
of sociological analysis, with the economic dimension apparently

overriding any others. In Wallerstein's initial accounts, at least, cultural and even political aspects of the world system played a fairly minor role. The local and the particular are vulnerable to effacement before the capitalist world system.

An alternative view does not picture the process of globalization as a kind of bulldozer whose caterpillar tracks have homogeneous effects wherever it travels. In this view, the world manifestly is not becoming one place, but, rather, is fracturing and splintering into tribal fragments and ethnic identities. Heterogeneity, not homogeneity, is the (dis)order of the day. Even economically, more goods and services are available, in greater variety and diversity than ever, and although giant telecommunications companies do account for much traffic in images and information, local cultures and keen competition ensure that those products are not uniform either. The flows move in different directions; not just from Europe or the USA, but from Japan and even – thinking now of the massive economic disparities and social divisions in global cities – from Brazil.[56] It is not hard to see how this view of globalization might be more congenial to those analysing postmodernity.

Postmodernity refers in part to an intensification of cultural contacts. Tourist travel, business exchanges, even the movement of refugees and emigrants, all create more opportunities for contact. These in turn contribute to an erosion of older boundaries and to doubts about traditional ways of doing things. At the same time, a global overproduction of images, objects, ideologies and differences, facilitated by CIT networks, and fuelled by the consumer capitalist system, throws further into question conventional, taken for granted realities. In this sense, global and postmodern circumstances are intertwined. Each contributes to the development of the other.

In this deregulated world, the emergence of unified political, cultural or religious systems seems unlikely. Although travel and the CITs may improve contacts between, say, Islamic or Christian groups with similar outlooks, local differences still are strongly felt. For instance, many western Muslims are unsympathetic to the fatwa against novelist Salman Rushdie, who had a price on his head for alleged blasphemy in *The Satanic Verses*. Or, to take a Christian example, a neo-Pentecostal movement dubbed the 'Toronto Blessing' touched down near the international airport in 1994, attracting many to its freshness and freedom of worship. While its impact differed in different places of the North Atlantic region, it was hardly felt in countries like Brazil. However, cognate Pentecostal movements now mushrooming in Rio and São Paulo amount to what one sociologist has called a 'globalization from below'. Though they too are in touch with others using new media, they are not English speaking, and usually comprise the urban poor, and minorities, thus affecting a very different social world from that of Toronto.[57]

The most promising way of approaching these issues is just to acknowledge that, at present, *both* unifying *and* fragmenting forces seem to be at work, and neither is currently more powerful. And while global processes, such as stock markets, telecommunications networks and airline operations, clearly do exist, each also has local nodes. Indeed, each local link is vital, and vulnerable. Diners at McDonald's in Tokyo or Moscow do not, after all, become Americans. They are Japanese and Russian burger-eaters.[58] Robertson has made fruitful use of the Japanese marketing concept, *dochakuka*, to suggest that the global and the local are always closely related. *Dochakuka* refers to adapting global outlooks and practices to local conditions, in a marketing context. This helps companies to try, not only to be more responsive to local situations, but to create new forms of consumption, such that the global and local are linked in a sort of ongoing dialectic. The English hybrid word for this is 'glocalization', and Robertson uses it to show not just how the local and the global, but also the economic and the cultural, are highly interdependent.

Other theorists, however, argue that global development is so far advanced that the time has come to abandon talk of modernity *and* postmodernity. Martin Albrow accepts the ambiguity in 'glocalization', while seeing it as one aspect of a 'global age' that really is going beyond modernity. He urges his readers to 'escape the stifling hold of the modern on the imagination. We live in our own time and the Global Age opens worlds up to us in unprecedented ways.'[59] For Albrow, changes currently signalled by the term 'postmodernity' are epochal, and, he says, continuing to use terms like postmodernity simply confuses the issue, because they still use the 'modern' referent. This is a stimulating thesis, because it obliges us to think hard about the historical question: is today's social transformation of such magnitude that we should just drop all hints of the old terminology?

It sounds convincing. Nevertheless, I hesitate. Not because modernity and its associated concepts have any particular personal world-view value for me (as Abrow rightly suggests it has for some theorists). Indeed, it is quite plausible to agree with Bruno Latour's insistence that 'we never were modern'.[60] In fact, part of my hesitation with 'the global age' position is that it could easily slip into a totalizing mode, rather like 'modernity' once did, one effect of which is that we might be blinded to the fact that globalization excludes and fragments some people as fast as it embraces and links others. The concept of postmodernity may be linked in illuminating ways with globalization, without taking that further step of exchanging the latter for the former. For better or worse, modernity has not gone away, despite the tectonic technological shifts taking place, and the unprecedented stretching of social relations enabled thereby.

Postindustrialism and postmodernity: an emerging agenda

Enough has been said, I think, to show that clear answers to the question posed earlier – 'New technology and society: beyond modernity?' – are hard to come by. That postmodern debates have displaced postindustrial ones within social theory does not mean that the problems associated with the former have been resolved. Indeed, they turn out to be more complex, if anything. But even if 'answers' are elusive, the question is a good one because it alerts us to some crucially important issues. In the final section of this chapter, which also sets the scene for the next, five aspects of the question are addressed: technological and social-cultural changes; centralization and dispersal; meaning and reality; homogeneity and heterogeneity; and the quests for critique.

Postindustrialism and information society, whose popularity peaked in the 1970s and 1980s, are concepts that feed on Enlightenment notions of progress through technological development. They propose that a new kind of social experience is emerging. Postmodernity rose to prominence as a social analytic concept during the 1980s and 1990s. It assumes technological change but in many accounts little space is accorded to connecting such developments with social transformations. I suggest that this is because 'progress', with which technology was once conceptually yoked, has largely been abandoned within postmodern analysis.

The fact that earlier beliefs in progress have proved empty does not render futile efforts either to understand or to guide technological development. Indeed, attempting these twin tasks is imperative today. As far as the former is concerned, some of the emphases within postindustrialism were not inappropriate. Bell's desire to find out just what proportion of the population is involved in one economic sector or another is a case in point. Today, for instance, more than half the US workforce may be considered to work within services and information sectors, including computing, television, media, advertising, journalism, accounting and publishing. While this may indicate the significance of 'information' to the economy, it also obscures the proportion still involved in menial, low-status positions.[61] At the same time, if postmodernity has more to do with consumers than workers, then the occupational structure will tell only part of the story. Also, Bell's initial focus on information may be giving way to one on communication – especially via computer networking – as the vital feature of these new times.

Similarly, the critique of postindustrialism is revealing for postmodernity. Two features stand out here. One is the deepening social and economic inequalities associated with the growth of electronics-based technologies; and the other is the greater potential for social control inherent in these technologies. Vattimo's analysis, other merits notwithstanding, is deficient here. The question of capitalist development simply cannot be sidestepped. The fact that his 'society of communication' has helped to erode some hierarchies does not mean it can be expected also to undermine capitalism, which still displays its old traits of domination and inequality. For many in poor countries, the global information society is another way of diverting basic resources from those who need them most.

The second aspect of the question concerning technologies and postmodernity is centralization and dispersal. The so-called modernist critique is fuelled by fear of the consequences of centralized power, especially that facilitated by the huge capacities of information technology. Big Brother, or a centralized panopticon prison, seems to lurk in the near future. But the evidence points the other way; no single omniscient power centre operates today, and in any case, much surveillance power is directed at classifying and guiding consumers, not at political repression. Poster's suggestion, however, that new forms of domination may be in the making, should not lightly be dismissed. Such 'new forms' remain to be explored.

So the critique of Adorno should not be supplanted so much as supplemented by that of Vattimo. Forms of power just as dangerous as those envisaged by Adorno may be augmented by the development of mass media based on new technology. But simultaneously, dispersed power may also result. The question again obliges us to do serious social analysis rather than merely to speculate. Even Poster's comments on the fate of dispersed selves within computer databases requires more investigation before we can confidently assume that this is a suitable framework from which to seek appropriate politics and policy proposals.

Third, to continue the communications theme, does meaning dissolve in a media-centred world? Without doubt, the status of 'reality' and 'meaning' is in radical question today. Morcover, this has occurred in part because of the so-called information revolution. Postmodernity is indeed a product of communicative development, as Vattimo says. But again, this does not mean that we are left with *only* images, signs without referents, any more than the dominant collage or montage style means we are beyond narratives. Coherence may still be sought in these images, these messages.

Baudrillard, probably best known for his extreme versions of this 'loss of meaning' thesis, achieved particular notoriety for declaring that the Gulf War had not happened. Now, no matter how far he can explain this by saying that *politically*, war did not happen, or whatever, he cannot be cleared from implying that the whole episode was simply unreal.[62] According to Baudrillard, unreality attended the war, the victory, the defeat and the ongoing Arab–Israeli negotiations. Computer and mass-media simulation – on both sides – was all there was. Now, these aspects of the Gulf War do represent a new stage in the history of warfare. Maybe it was the first postmodern war. But what did Baudrillard mean? To cling to irony to the extent of apparently denying that blood stained the sand and bereaved families mourned is surely irresponsible. Has Baudrillard spent too long in front of the TV? Or did he really intend his provocative shock tactics to promote the recovery of some last shreds of humanity from the banality of mediation?

Closely connected with the question of new technologies and meaning is that of global homogeneity or heterogeneity. Are the CITs helping to forge the one world of a global village, with converging economic and political life; or are these exploding into little fragments of niche marketing and tribal dispute? The evidence of the later twentieth century suggests that, rather than one process being predominant, both are occurring with more-or-less equal impact, depending on the context. Thus the global situation might better be considered as an arena, facilitated by new communications, in which cultures, polities and economies mix and clash. The linear process of unification, which European and American modernities found so attractive, gives way to a state of affairs where local differences actually become clearer, as once remote groups become neighbours, and are obliged to come to terms with such differences.[63] How they will do so is still very much an open question.

This brings us finally, then, to the quest for critique. The question can be put simply. Is the Babel of communicative society[64] – now enlarged to a global range – a situation to be welcomed for its liberating potential or resisted as disintegrative and destructive of human relationships? Habermas offers a modern view: human sociality and solidarity is pursued within communicative rationality. Hermeneutics is the way forward to mutual understanding and undistorted communication. We can know what it is to be 'human' and that this means we are 'naturally' intersubjective and communicative. Against this is the view of Nietzsche and Heidegger, that an ethic of interpretation follows from the recognition of nihilism. This would recognize provenance – where we are coming from – rather than any positive destination or future emerging from the present.[65]

From the ethical stance must flow the political options, and the question of postmodernity certainly raises both in new ways. I shall argue in Chapter 6 that neither option mentioned here fully does justice to the problems raised by postmodernity. For the present, I conclude with this: the new technologies of information and communication, while in themselves bringing about neither the postindustrial nor the postmodern society – let alone hope for the resolution of contemporary crises[66] – are nonetheless profoundly implicated in contemporary transformations of world. Without them, the now universal existence of consumerism and consumer cultures would be impossible. To these we turn next.

Consumerism and Beyond: The Shape(lessness) of Things to Come

'Hey, pass it on, misplaced your faith,
and the candyman's gone'
Bruce Cockburn, 'Candyman's Gone'

'Why is LA, why are the deserts so fascinating?' asks Baudrillard. His answer, that 'you are delivered from all depth there', gets us quickly to the heart of this chapter. America, for Baudrillard, is a cultural desert, and LA 'an outer hyperspace, with no origin, no reference points'.[1] Or perhaps one reference point remains: consumption. This vision of the 'pathetic postmodern human' is just that, insists Stjepan Meštrović, because Baudrillard puts the consumer centre stage without any props or script by which to decipher the drama of consuming. Though Baudrillard raids Thorstein Veblen's classic nineteenth-century profile of American conspicuous consumption, he dumps its very driving motor: critique.[2]

If the processes of modernization gave us the social condition of modernity, with its answering echoes of modernism and antimodernism in experimental arts, then how do we understand postmodernizing processes, postmodernity and postmodernism? Shifts within capitalism and industrialism following the post-war consumer boom in the advanced societies spawned what Bell called postindustrialism. But as we saw, these changes are now taken to

be more significant as the material and social springboard for postmodern conditions. So postmodernization has to do with the
altered industrial landscape, with its mobile, flexible production,
the upheaval in the occupational structure that places services and
so-called information workers in a majority, and a compressed
world, where new technologies enable not only new methods of
production but different ways of relating socially.

What we have not yet discussed in any depth is the rise of consumerism, and the possibility that in the contemporary creation of
the new consumer lies a crucial clue for understanding postmodernity and postmodernism. In this chapter, then, the main motif is consumption, seen both as the linchpin of a dominant cultural code and
as a putative novel social condition. What may be fairly obvious in
a world of rock videos, theme parks and shopping malls also seeps
into domains once thought somewhat beyond the market, such as
science, religion, gender, ethnicity and the human body. Do the
technologies of communication collude with the consumer culture
to create a postmodern condition? And what are the possible consequences for lifestyles, or for values such as authority, solidarity,
identity or hope?

Remember that a major mark of the modern era is the ability to
adapt, to find new ways of producing, communicating, governing
and so on. Although Marx was right to note the erosive tendencies
of capitalism – or of modernity in general – just as the solid melted
into air, some alternatives evolved to substitute for the 'solid'.
Belief in Providence, that once sustained confidence about the
future, found a surrogate in Progress. Similarly, Revelation waned
in social significance, at least among certain influential elites, only
to find its place taken by Reason. In the early twentieth century,
modernism, seen in cubism, and the 'machine aesthetic' of Le
Corbusier and the Bauhaus, still offered positive ways forward,
even though surrealism and stream-of-consciousness writing hinted
at the limits of Reason, faintly foreshadowing the postmodern. The
city as machine would make perfect sense of the modern situation,
creating conditions for a rational and progressive future.

But it is precisely this assumption, that modernity has endless
capacities for adaptation through a merging of rationality and
progress, which today is challenged head on. Habermas calls it a
'legitimation crisis'. Not only are old institutions and authority
centres – religion, royalty, tradition – criticized and contested. Even

the metanarratives of modernity turn out to have limited shelf-life. Not only do truth and justice appear rather questionable concepts but the reduction of everything to exchange values seems to iron out all 'lasting' values. The fear, for many, is this: will the postmodern condition leave us in a permanent flux of relativity, where all is subject only to the arbitrary machinations of the marketplace?

I begin with the much discussed symptoms of postmodernism in consumer culture – the city as a 'giant screen',[3] Disneyland as utopia – and try to characterize some of its major traits. Then I ask the sociological questions: what does this apparent shift portend? How does it connect with other aspects of contemporary societies? Is postmodernism a cultural reflex of late capitalism, or does it bespeak a new social order beyond capitalism? The new Babel of varied voices to be heard on all sides could be understood either way. But if postmodern consumer culture demands analysis beyond conventional Marxism and sociology, what sort of analysis and what sort of critique are called for?

Consumer culture

Close to where I write this, changes in Princess Street in Kingston, Ontario, illustrate well the shift to consumer culture. Where once ship's chandlers, butchers, bakers and cabinet-makers sold their wares, now numerous fashionable clothing stores, restaurants, street cafés, wholefood shops, camera, computer and hi-fi equipment outlets, banks, trust companies and travel agents ply their trades. In the summer-time a tourist train wends its way through the 'limestone city' streets, imparting snippets of local history to visitors. Included in the tour is the Italian villa home of Canada's first prime minister, Sir John A. MacDonald, and views across the bay to Old Fort Henry, 'Canada's original theme park'.

The postmodern is rightly associated with a society where consumer lifestyles and mass consumption dominate the waking lives of its members. Fashion and taste are eclectic – summer activities in Kingston include everything from 'Shakespeare in the park' to *Jurassic Park* in the movie theatre, and from windsurfing to (mock) paddle-steamer cruises on the water. Opportunities are endless, and the quest for new market niches, constant. Services and leisure industries abound, along with signals from every imaginable – and unimaginable, virtual reality – medium. No wonder some who still hold to a hierarchy of values, or who cherish chronology or a coherent story-line suggest that reality itself is unsettled, undermined, so that, eventually, meaning itself evaporates. Equally, it is no wonder that nostalgia also abounds, for the heroic heritage of British military pageant or of confident Canadian confederation.

Several things may be noted here. First, consumption, and a focus on the production of needs and wants, is central. Everything is commodified, and this process is reinforced by constant TV advertising. Adequate funds to support consumer lifestyles are presupposed, along with sufficient leisure time to indulge them. As it happens, Princess Street also marks an old social divide; conspicuous consumers to the south and the less well-off to the north. Second, the city is still the site of cultural shifts. The altered emphasis from the economic and functional to the cultural and aesthetic is clearly visible in urban areas; any move to the postmodern is metropolitan. Third, consumer culture may be connected with other more general cultural phenomena. Not just artistic and consumer goods, but intellectual and even religious ones become subject to the market, which resists both monopoly and hierarchy. This is bad news for 'authoritative' pronouncements from academic, religious or political sources, although defensive responses to it may help create a cultural climate conducive to religious revival or lingering Marxist utopianism.[4] The first two aspects round out this section, while the third is the subject of the next.

Whether through the mushrooming of massive shopping malls, more and more tightly targeted junk mail, or the cacophony of commercials on TV, few in the advanced societies can be unaware that we inhabit consumer cultures. Or perhaps consumer *culture*, because we can now watch *Dallas*, eat Big Macs and drink Coke anywhere. Perhaps not. Coke may contain the same ingredients, and come with the same familiar red label, but its social meanings still vary with time and location. Shopping, no longer a necessary evil or a domestic chore, now exhibits itself as a leisure pursuit. To choose a day out at the shopping mall is clearly considered fun by many, especially if it is a climate controlled, theme-park inspired, total experience like those to be enjoyed at the Gateshead Metro Centre in England, the West Edmonton Mall in Canada, or the Toison d'Or in Dijon, France.

Television and consumer culture belong together, although it is a mistake to impute simple causal status to the former. They have grown symbiotically since the Second World War. As Baudrillard suggests, the postmodern splits away from the modern when the production of demand – of consumers – becomes central. And TV is all about 'the production of needs and wants, the mobilization of desire and fantasy, of the politics of distraction'.[5] For Baudrillard, the Marxist insistence on mode-of-production analysis is simply inadequate to comprehend the consumer society. Consumer objects are actually a system of signs that differentiate the population. Signifiers, like TV ads, 'float' freely, with only the loosest connection with actual objects. Think of the Marlboro man, the 'real thing', 'if it's not Kelloggs on the packet it's not Kelloggs in the packet', beer that reaches parts that others don't, the 'united colors' of Benetton, Nike's 'Just do it!', BMW's 'Ultimate driving machine', and the Levi denim label. Their purpose is only to incite desire. From this kind of 1970s analysis, it was a short step to Baudrillard's 1980s world of simulacra, of hyperreality, where the *only* 'reality' is TV ads and other signifiers. One does not have to accept Baudrillard *tout court* to see the importance of his view that the new languages of TV and electronic media take us into consumer culture and also beyond Marxism.[6]

Certainly it is hard to find clear cultural boundary markers today. The rise of consumerism and of TV viewing has accelerated the 'implosion' of reality, obscuring previously cherished distinctions between highbrow and lowbrow, between the culture of the elite and the culture of the masses. History becomes 'heritage' and the musty museum a 'hands-on' multimedia experience. Think of Kingston's Fort Henry, where the razzmatazz of redcoated soldiers marching with muskets is the main attraction. BBC Radio 3 in the UK and CBC Radio Two in Canada now carry jazz and rock music that would have been anathema to 'classical' music buffs in the pre-1960s era.

In the world of fiction, 'contemporary' novels and science fiction are harder to tell apart. No longer using techniques to help us grasp and even conquer complexity, writers now lead us deeper into their confusion about who they are and how to respond to strange and split worlds of surfaces and signifiers.[7] Or, like Jane Urquhart's *The Underpainter*, they start with realist landscapes, then carefully paint out the 'realism'. Rather than warning about fearful futures, writers like Thomas Pynchon offer genealogical accounts of the near past and present. Not that fear is absent. Slothrop's paranoid vision, in

Gravity's Rainbow, is worthy of Foucault himself. But this is dystopia now, not even in the 2019 of *Blade Runner*.

Much of this fading-out of reality takes place in the city. The path from cinema to TV and then video was taken first in urban contexts. The youth culture of the 1960s, with its new-found spending power for fashion, motor bikes and pop music, also started in the city. The deindustrialization of cities turned them into centres of consumption – hence the mega-malls and museums. And hence also the investment in image, a factor crucial to the success of cities that have lost their manufacturing or financial base. But cities are also sites where social images are on display, where advertising and promotion is most intense, and where the conspicuous acts of consumption are most significant. Latest looks, new waves, states-of-the-art are all to be found in the city. Style circulates swiftly, with occasional nostalgic raids on the more distant past.[8]

Does the city thus transform itself into the postmodern? Both the premodern city, such as Venice, with its ancient buildings, landmarks and Renaissance architecture, rooted in history and tradition, and the modern city, such as New York, with its planned grid of streets, functional design and high-rise buildings of glass and concrete, must now make room for the postmodern city – Los Angeles perhaps? In the USA the solid did not exactly melt into air, but was bulldozed to make way for the new. Robert Moses cheerfully flattened older New York to carve out spaces for his freeways. And Christopher Jencks proposes that we date postmodernity from when the machine-for-living Pruitt-Igoe housing complex in St Louis was demolished at 3.32 pm on 15 July 1972.[9]

This is how Disneyland becomes the popular architectural utopia. The strip of tarmac, bordered with bright neon signs, seducing all and sundry to the pleasures of consumption – whether food, furniture or film, it matters not – is the first indication that you are driving into a North American city. (I mean any American city, not only Celebration, Florida, which is the town actually built by Disney.) The lure and attraction of each display, each experience, must outdo the last. Art and everyday life are mixed up in a *mélange* of shapes and images. Once such symbols delineated specific youth subcultures, but now, if it is not quite the case that everyone is a teenager, at least everyone has their market slot. Grey-power is the obvious new contender for marketability in rapidly ageing populations. Play and entertainment, consumption and the 'tourist gaze'[10] are what the postmodern city is about. 'Involvement' and 'participation' are vital; having watched the *son et lumière* at Fort Henry, donning a military cap and trying to march in step is the alternative to dallying in the gift shop. Baudelaire's *flâneurs*, whether or not they have succumbed to riding the remote – channel-hopping – are still in the city.

More than one commentator cites Los Angeles as the world's first truly postmodern city. The vast oceanside metropolis has a huge share of high-tech occupations, plus low-paid service and manufacturing jobs. But it has gone through such rapid (selective) deindustrialization and reconstitution that Edward Soja calls it 'the paradigmatic window through which to see the last half of the twentieth century'.[11] Yet it is hard to focus on this constantly moving, fragmentary urban flow that is everywhere, global.

LA houses Star Wars technologists and film stars, but each in their own (guarded) enclaves. It has squalid slums and gentrified midmodern neighbourhoods. It boasts a large airport, LAX, and officeblock, hotel and shopping mall corridors. It sprawls heterogeneously over many square miles, but lacks an identifiable centre. If there is a centre, says Soja, it is the Bonaventure Hotel, 'an amazingly storeyed architectural symbol of the splintered labyrinth that stretches sixty miles around it'. Mini-cities make it up with nostalgic memories of other geographies in their names: Venice, Manhattan Beach, Ontario, Westminster. Everything is vivid, simultaneous, interconnected. A postmodern, depthless, soft city.[12] Was *Blade Runner* wrongly dated in the twenty-first century?

LA also exemplifies what Mike Davis calls the 'bad edge of postmodernity'.[13] Living there, people are caught in a new limbo between the local and the global, present in modernity but amplified today. The global is expressed not only in the world-wide distribution of Hollywood movies, but in the risks of radicalized modernity associated with, among other things, precarious employment – mainly of Hispanics and Asians – in post-Fordist flexible transnational industries. Such labourers are also contained in their spaces by the high-tech control mechanisms of electronic surveillance, and lawns sprouting 'armed response' signs. And as the 1992 riots demonstrated, racism, hatred, poverty and despair are frighteningly close to the surface.

On a personal level, not just the deunionized and marginal, but the yuppies as well, experience new tensions of identity and selfhood. In common with others in what Giddens calls the 'high modern' period, individuals seek to express themselves in 'free' consumer choices, guided by the lifestyle packages of the advertisers. Thus 'the project of self becomes translated into one of the possession of desired goods and the pursuit of artificially framed styles of life'.[14] Despite his hesitation to call this 'postmodern', Giddens sees this consumption in the mass market, with its reshaping of the conditions of everyday life, as a 'novel phenomenon'. From TV ads to soap operas, mediated experience is involved in contemporary constructions of the self. The global and the local have never before interacted in such intense ways in routine, daily experience.

Varied voices

Consumerism knows no boundaries. It neither respects domains once immune from its effects, nor supports existing markers of cultural territory. As Philip Sampson notes, 'Once established, such a culture of consumption is quite undiscriminating and everything becomes a consumer item, including meaning, truth and knowledge.'[15] Product image, style and design take over from modern metanarratives the task of conferring meaning. 'Things fall apart', said W. B. Yeats, presciently; 'the centre cannot hold'.[16] So the symbolic centrelessness of LA becomes a metaphor for postmodern consumer culture in general; all is fragmented, heterogeneous, dispersed, plural – and subject to consumer choices.

The populism of shopping malls and TV news extends to other areas. Empowerment and self-actualization become important. Hierarchy crumbles under the pressure of new management techniques – in Silicon Valley T-shirts and jeans replace formal suits – of women's movements, of new ethnic and sexual awareness. Intellectuals are demoted from legislative to interpretive tasks, as the seminar, not the lecture becomes the preferred medium of academic exchange. Architecture and town planning become matters for participation and consultation with clients, not expert blueprinting, and clergy find themselves encouraging higher levels of 'lay' involvement in the traditional churches.

As the overarching ideals of the modern era give way to the fluctuating, varied voices of the possibly postmodern, so any hopes of holding to a single way of being or a unified cosmos dwindle away. Or so it seems to some. In the realm of religion, what Peter Berger calls a 'heretical imperative' exerts itself, that denies unique truth and obliges one person's doctrine to be another's doubt. In the scientific scene, the old certainties of method and experiment dissolve as reason-based 'truth' is dismantled. And what was once a self-assured regime of patriarchal privilege is steadily undermined by feminism, an other voice, insisting that hu*man* is not the end of the story.

Values and beliefs seem to lose any sense of coherence, let alone continuity, in the world of consumer choice, multiple media and globalized (post)modernity. Berger's concept of the 'heretical imperative' suggests how, increasingly, traditional religious views are subject to abrasive encounter with modern, secularizing tendencies.[17] The vertigo of relativity, the abyss of uncertainty, are its results. But this also is a consequence of a world where choice reigns supreme; hesitation, anxiety and doubt seem to be the price paid for that sense of choice.[18] The shift from fate to choice, or from providence to progress, that was supposed to be so liberating, appears to have a darker side, which veils the further spiral into nihilism.

Consumer choice may infiltrate religious and church life. Reginald Bibby's Canadian study, *Fragmented Gods*, argues that religion 'has become a neatly packaged consumer item – taking its place among other commodities that can be bought or bypassed according to one's consumption whims'.[19] From being a central, life-informing and life-influencing phenomenon of Canadian social and public experience, Christianity has largely succumbed to consumerism, as a minority leisure pursuit. One might also note that today's 'spiritualities' also tend to be centred on choice. New Age networks have little in common but the desire to discover the divine in ourselves through a great diversity of routes. Native religious ideas nestle naturally next to Eastern mysticism and ancient goddess paganism. No creed channels belief, only 'spirit guides' that lead in reassuring, inoffensive directions.[20] Though I use Canadian examples, such processes are in train elsewhere as well.

Before we too quickly conclude that the heretical imperative means all major belief systems disintegrate, however, it is worth noting that celebrated cases of heresy relate to religions of great longevity. Martin Scorcese's *Last Temptation of Christ* and Salman Rushdie's *The Satanic Verses*, after all, are seen by segments of the faithful as attacks on Christianity and Islam. The capacity of ancient premodern religions to continue, revive and even flourish in contemporary conditions should not be underestimated.[21] In a sense, heresy serves to demonstrate the vitality of religion. Doubt may be institutionalized in late-modern or postmodern situations, but this itself may encourage a parallel move towards the reassertion of faith, and not only in its fundamentalist forms either, as well as towards rehabilitating modern metanarratives.[22]

The pluralizing and fragmenting effects evident within contemporary consumer societies test traditional conceptions of truth. Whereas tolerance was once believed to be founded in unique truth, the irony is that pluralism – which that tolerance permitted – now requires that truth be abandoned. The English Act of Toleration (1689) was intended to end post-Reformation factional conflict. Churches supported the Act because of their 'confidence in the ability of the Truth to vindicate itself without the instruments of state coercion'.[23] Today's tolerance, in contrast, is tissue-thin and tears away to reveal ugly and sometimes violent confrontations at the smallest provocation. Extreme acts carried out in the name of political correctness are but one illustration.

Another sphere in which truth is contested is that of science. Again, in early modern times a concept of divine truth underlay efforts to 'think thoughts after God's'. But, transmuted into the quest of empirical 'truth' available to the senses alone, this concept of truth made itself vulnerable to eventual dismantling. As Nietzsche said, the 'will to truth' in science has been 'called into question'. And Lyotard observes today that 'science plays its own game; it is incapable of legitimating the other language games . . . above all, it is incapable of legitimating itself'.[24] No sure methodological foundation is available any longer; postmodernists claim that the certitudes of science lie in ruins. Indeed, knowledge as moderns thought they knew it is dissolved; universal accounts of the world are simply not possible any more. Picking up this gauntlet inaugurated the 'science wars' of the 1990s.[25]

The best known early intervention in post-war philosophy of science is Thomas Kuhn's. He demonstrated that scientific 'revolutions' take place, not just when incontrovertible new evidence is found, but when assumptions alter. Scientific theories depend on underlying 'paradigms' by which the world is understood.[26] Even the work of white-coated scientists labouring in labs with their test-tubes and data was not beyond critique. Paul Feyerabend insisted that data itself is theory-dependent, as is the very concept of what *is* data. And the fate of science was finally sealed, in this account, by the Lyotard–Foucault–Derrida assault.[27] The linguistic gap between description and reality and the interplay of power and discourse mean that science is suspect on more than one count: oversimplifying, it is either sheer surface or mere power.

Accepting that no scientific foundations exist to legitimate thought or politics is part of the popular postmodern position. Vattimo declares that this difference, this disorientation, is our human state. The multiple realities of the local and the limited are our world, and it could be liberating to discover them. Richard Rorty, taking his cues from Foucault, derides the dangerous deception of attachment to ' "systematic", scientific, representational reality' and offers instead hermeneutic or 'edifying' discourse that acknowledges plurality as a given.[28] To be suspicious of epistemology, and of science which ends up objectifying human beings, is one thing, however; to offer an alternative is another. Rorty thinks he will take philosophers beyond the either/or of modernist inquiry but this does leave a difficulty: what next? If the 'True and Right are matters of social practice'[29] then surely a lot more should be discovered about those practices?

The most public skirmish in the 'science wars' occurred in 1996 when Alan Sokal, a New York University physicist, had a spoof article entitled 'Transgressing the Boundaries: Towards a Transformative Hermeneutics of Quantum Gravity', published in *Social Text*, a cultural studies journal. In response, another physicist, Steven Weinberg, capitalized on this coup by explaining to the *New York Review of Books* that 'if we ever discover intelligent creatures on some distant planet, we will find that we and they have discovered the same laws'.[30] Universal science lives! Ten years earlier, however, Bruno Latour had argued that instability characterizes those 'laws'. The public face of science, with its emphasis on firmness and transcultural reliability, is always accompanied by another face, in which private controversy, uncertainty and debate abound. He likened the trials of strength between such 'objectivity' and 'subjectivity' to the 'balance of power between two armies'. The relative rhetorical power of contending collective forces determines the outcome.[31]

If we take the case of feminism, the delineation of social practices comes immediately to the foreground. Some feminists observe, with justification, that their struggle to make 'malestream' science recognize its inherent bias – its paradigm – has hastened the eclipse of empiricism. Male models, metaphors and methods abound in science,[32] where female ones could substitute for or, better, interact with them. At the same time, feminists frequently hesitate before the brink of full postmodernism. Rejecting foundationalism need not entail the abandonment of systematic social critique of women's subordination to men.[33] Who would accept that the discourse of patriarchy could ever be edifying, any more than could that of cannibalism or torture? The moral vacuity – offence! – of such views refuses to remain hidden.

For Susan Hekman, postmodernity is Janus-faced.[34] The postmodern mood, like much feminism, militates against Enlightenment epistemologies, a trait particularly strong in debates over the human sciences. But few feminists describe themselves as postmodern. Why? Because older feminisms share the Enlightenment commitment to emancipation that is also seen in liberal humanism and Marxism. Hekman's resolution of this is a mutually informed feminism and postmodernism. This position could never suppose that there is an 'essential' female nature, but neither could it allow postmodernism – to whose discourses many contributors have been male – to persist with its gendered analyses.

While some feminists optimistically see in the postmodern critique an opportunity to challenge again the old hierarchies of colour, gender, class and race,[35] others are less sure. These others warn of the dangers of embracing doctrines that seem to leave only a sense of powerlessness, even escapism, or that fail to disclose the basis of their implicit moral stance. Even in a world awash with relativism, we can be sure of some things; for example, oppression is wrong, and some things can and should be done to end it.[36] Writing on the morning I had just returned from a memorial to the Montreal massacre of 14 women engineering students at the Ecole Polytechnique, this seemed painfully obvious.

What is true for the struggle against patriarchy is also true for others attempting to find authentic post-foundational starting points for social criticism. The postmodern context, with its emphasis on individual choice and consumer preferences, when mixed with epistemological doubt and pluralism, creates a heady cocktail that seems quickly to befuddle and paralyse. At best, only local rationales, or subgroup standpoints seem available as means of discernment and choice. It is hard to see how any (post)modern society can in any sense become a desirable habitat without coming to terms with this. However, one further issue is also raised by the issue of gender and sexuality. If the 'essential' woman or man is

hard to define, what of the human? Since before the Enlightenment, being (hu)man was taken to be 'the measure of all things'.
Might even this melt into air?

The body, the borg, and the beast

In a world of increasingly available bio- and info-technologies, the
human body itself is not immune from colonization within consumer culture. It is not merely that cosmetic alterations to the body
are possible, that new reproductive technologies create novel
choices, or that some believe they can escape the body altogether in
cyberspace or virtual reality. Nor are we discussing variations on
Turing's test for whether or not machines truly can think. Each of
these assumes that the distinctively *human* body can still be known,
such that it can be told apart from the beasts (the early modern preoccupation) or the machine (the later modern concern). Defining
and experiencing the body in a consumer world is less a matter of
anatomical precision and unambiguous uniqueness, and more a
matter of decision, doubt, and debate.

The body has become the site of style in postmodern culture. It
is plastic, malleable, subject to alteration, mutation, enhancement.
In a consumer culture the body can be moulded into any desired
appearance.[37] From teenage nose and eyebrow rings to the elabor-
ate ornamenting, carving and modelling of cosmetic chameleons
like Michael Jackson or the French dancer Orlan, who models
herself on favoured features from a number of figures, modification
and sculpture is performed on the body itself. Bodies may be
'improved' as in any other industrial process, either at an early
stage, using reproductive technologies, or later, using surgery,
hormone treatments, or chemical applications. The body may even
take centre stage as the real 'me', as being equivalent to the self.[38]

Of course, bodies may also be consumed in the cinema or
through the television screen. *Pulp Fiction*'s violent portrayal of the
malleable body is no less postmodern than the obsession with
bodily enhancement. And the sight of war-broken bodies, such as
the infamous Vietnamese girl covered with burning napalm, Iraqis
incinerated during the 1991 Gulf War, or beheaded corpses being
eaten by pigs and dogs in Bosnia, also took their ambiguous place
in the later twentieth century's televised stories of the body. But as
bodies become consumer items, they are literally consumed (on the

screen) in a film dealing with the aftermath of an air crash in the Andes – *Alive* – or in the refined cannibalism of Peter Greenaway's *The Cook, The Thief, His Wife, and Her Lover.*

None of these scenes, however horrifying, obliges the viewer to participate or even to think about the consequences of violence, whether 'real' or 'fictional'. As Kevin Robins observes, 'The screen that provides us with information about the world's realities is also a screen against the shock of seeing and knowing about those realities.'[39] This telling comment could also be used of another electronically mediated means of encountering (or avoiding) other bodily experiences, only this one admits to no 'real world' connections. Virtual reality, with its best known selling point, cybersex, appears to promise the possibility of transcending the body, along with all that compromises its experiences – weakness, sickness, suffering and death. Pleasure and security is guaranteed to the consumer; cybersex is safe, and the solipsistic cocoon contains no uncomfortable or challenging situations. At least while the plug is in the electrical socket.

Bodies: enhancement, experiences, encounters – all are offered to the consumer. To some, the postmodern body may seem to evade reality, as defined in conventional, modern terms. But to others, new potential lies right here for prying open the grip of such modern definitions of bodily reality. When the boundaries are blurring, whether by medical, electronic, or other means, the body becomes contested terrain. Technological transformations may be grasped, not as flights from reality, but as the means of creating new bodily and social realities, unimpeded by modern categories and constraints. Virtual reality is just one aspect of possible prosthetic extensions provided by genetic, medical, electronic and other technologies. Machines may enter or attach to the body, to improve everything from memory to mobility. 'Personal' computing takes new turns as performance-enhancing gadgets upgrade the consumer body, rather as they do in cars or homes.[40] And in August 1998 Kevin Warwick, at Reading University, took this to its obvious conclusion when he had a radio receiver and chips implanted under his skin. Computers can now communicate directly with this 'cyborg', wherever he is.[41]

Creating continuity rather than disjuncture between machine and body may have far-reaching potential for breaking out of modern modes of thinking and being. For Donna Haraway, the 'cyborg identity' represents the chance to go beyond gender, to delight in the confusion of boundaries and to take responsibility for their construction. Playing with personae on the Internet is but one small step into the imaginative world of cyborg identity, where the scope for emancipation is seemingly endless. As Haraway says, 'Bodies . . . are not born; they are made.'[42] Discourses of the body construct it; for example through Romantic notions of harmony, or through modern medical anatomical description. So why not the 'postmodern body', one rendering of which is cyborgs, the 'compounds of hybrid techno-organic embodiment and textuality'?[43] Haraway insists that she wishes to escape neither death nor reality, but rather to demonstrate possibilities for another order of signification. Her trademark slogan? 'Cyborgs for earthly survival!'

Even if cyborgs are not your thing, the idea that body discourses may be constraining is a common theme within contemporary feminisms. Cultural depictions of female bodies have in this view been held too long in the sway of rigid patriarchal codes. Women, who have not been permitted to be themselves, now assert this as a right. But not only women. Familiar heterosexual stereotypes are widely questioned, such that lesbian, gay and bisexual practices and identities are advocated as a means of expressing what has been suppressed or rejected by the dominant discourses. This way the body becomes a visible carrier of self-identity. Supported as a form of self-expression by the liberal democratic state, what once was condemned as perversion is now not only tolerated but celebrated as welcome diversity.[44]

Are there limits to this? Well, if the idea is that postmodern bodies and sexual identities are the product of freely chosen consumer decisions, then Judith Butler, for one, has her doubts. In *Bodies that Matter*, she resists the notion that 'constructed' means artificial or dispensable. While deconstructing *both* heterosexuality *and* homosexuality, and moving well beyond all classifications based on male and female anatomy, she sees construction as 'constitutive constraint'.[45] Sex, gender and sexuality may be deconstructed, chimes in Terry Lovell, but they cannot be dispensed with.[46] After all, the heterosexual matrix is universal, though always located in different histories and cultural contexts, and the pertinent question of 'construction' may be how to overcome domination and exploitation both for those within and outside such relationships. But don't hold your breath, warns Manuel Castells. The struggle between power and identity in the body-battleground does not necessarily liberate, and society may become 'simply a supermarket of personal fantasies, in which individuals will consume each other rather than produce themselves'.[47]

In this way and many others, the status of the body is central to the debate over postmodernity. The body is subject to (tele)visual violence in a dangerous world, is pulled in different directions in disputes over its constitution, and is a key resource for commercial exploitation. For Philip Mellor and Chris Shilling, our times are characterized by the 'baroque body' that faces two directions at once, both cognitive and sensual.[48] The latter was previously a feature of medieval embodiment, where the world of angels, demons and spirits was a way of coping with life experienced as 'nasty, brutish and short'. Protestantism helped furnish a more cognitive cast to the body, removing from the flesh much superstition and sacred significance, and allowing it to be examined, dissected and classified by science. The word came into play much more, and with that the mind enthroned itself decisively over the all too often merely sinful body of flesh.

The baroque body may be seen, for instance, in virtual reality, where the cognitive control motif vies with the sensual, fleshly aspects of electronic experience.[49] But the world of electronic experiences may also contribute to the sense of the disintegration of the self, and the breakdown of social coherence into tribal differences and self-referential identity struggles. If cognitive control represents one of the few remaining vestiges of Protestant influence, it is unlikely to be sufficient to counteract the collapse of many aspects of modern culture under the weight of their own contradictions.[50] What then of the future of embodied selves and identities? How will the contradictions of the baroque body be played out? If, as Haraway argues, knowledge of bodies is 'situated', then what count as 'situations' from which knowledge(s) may be produced?[51] Whatever the answers, the moral question of the human body will be a central one in the twenty-first century, and may well outlive the debate over postmodernity.

The all-consuming society?

It must be clear by now that the (post)modern is more than a shift in the structure of sensibility, that could be dismissed as merely 'cultural', and thus potentially irrelevant to the ongoing life of contemporary societies. Postmodernism in novels, films, music and architecture is highly significant both in its own right and as a mirror held up to social and political changes. The question is: what is the nature of those changes? Certainly, meaning may be threatened *à la* Baudrillard, and discourse altered *à la* Lyotard, but hyperreality or linguistics hardly does justice to the social question.

For Marxists like Fredric Jameson, postmodernism is unmasked as the cultural logic of late capitalism. The production of culture has been integrated into commodity production in general, so that struggles once limited to production now spill over into cultural spheres. Everything from the definition of taste to countercultural movements of the 1960s could be understood under this rubric.[52] For David Harvey, in his elegant reading of the postmodern condition, we are indeed in a time of tremendous fragmentation and flux. But this flux can still be viewed within a historical materialist framework, where the accent is on post-Fordism, flexible production . . . and capitalism's 'inner logic'.[53]

This sort of talk is too hard for others to swallow. Neither the diminution of the issues to the 'merely cultural' nor their diversion back into modernist Marxism will do. To another group of analysts, Marxism can no longer supply all the answers. But, they insist, a sociology of postmodernity is still worth pursuing, even one that still takes some cues from Marxism. Among these, I find the 'intimations of postmodernity' noted by Zygmunt Bauman most compelling.[54] Having disposed of views that consider the postmodern as either a culture-and-personality crisis, somehow floating free of the rest of society, or as a social-system-in-crisis, in which postmodernity is a pathological aberration, Bauman concludes that in the late twentieth century we are witnessing the start of a new type of society.

Concisely put, Bauman believes that in present-day society, consumer conduct is moving steadily 'into the position of, simultaneously, the cognitive and moral focus of life, the integrative bond of the society, and the focus of systemic management'.[55] The position once held by work, in modern capitalism, is now taken by 'consumer freedom geared to the consumer market'. Issues of control, the right to self-manage, are displaced from factory to store. Consuming, not working, becomes the 'hub around which the life-world rotates'. Pleasure, once seen as the enemy of capitalist industriousness, now performs an indispensable role.

The wheels of the system are powered by consumption; credit-card junkies are a boon. And at a social level, pressure to spend comes from symbolic rivalry and from the need to construct our self(-image) through the acquisition of the distinctive and different. Coercion can safely be superseded; as Pierre Bourdieu says, seduction takes over as the means of social control and integration.[56] (A downtown Kingston store sign bids us 'come in for the fun of it'.) Capitalism not only remains intact, but it is stronger, and can look forward to a favoured future. Only those who fail to consume, who are insufficiently integrated into the consumer market, need fear the old panoptical methods of surveillance and social control that once kept order in the factory and the street. If the new social management cannot seduce them, only then might it resort to repression.

Very importantly for our earlier discussion, the implication of Bauman's argument is that traditional mechanisms for finding political consensus and legitimation can freely be allowed to fall into disrepair. Cultural hegemony is redundant. With consumer choice established as the market-lubricated axis on which system reproduction, social integration and individual life-worlds smoothly revolve, 'cultural variety, hereogeneity of styles and differentiation of belief-systems become conditions of its success'. What appear in other accounts as purely artistic or cultural phenomena – from New Wave to New Age – uncoupled from serious social analysis, thus reappear in Bauman's version as the logical complements of consumer society.

Now, much could be – and has been – said about this breathtaking sociology of postmodernity. I shall not rehearse the arguments here, save to pick up one question raised already in this chapter: what form would *critique* take within such an analysis? For Bauman, who once argued for a socialist sociology, the approach must be reappraised. The issues cannot be confronted using terms derived merely from postmodernity, or, for that matter, from modernity. The capitalist–communist split was a mirage; a squabble *within* modernity. Both, after all, accept the doctrine of progress. Yet Bauman is impatient with someone like Baudrillard, who frames the world in a TV screen. Impossible, retorts Bauman: 'To many people, much in their life is anything but simulation. They need to sink their teeth into some quite real bread before they abandon themselves to munching images.'[57]

Bauman's critique seems to centre on identifying with the sufferers, the oppressed. And he does take consumerism to task for its 'duplicity'. It promises what it cannot deliver: universal happiness. And it makes false claims in solving the problem of freedom by reducing it to *consumer* freedom: are no other kinds left? This is no socialist critique, he insists. He sees his position as informed by much broader, western, Enlightenment values.[58] A case could be made for dating them earlier: Old Testament prophets such as Amos inveighed against exactly such deceptive pseudo-virtues, on the grounds that a providential (= provider) God requires that all share freely in enough of creation's bounty to lead dignified lives.

Others see battle breaking out on many fronts at once. New social movements, spawned in the 1960s, comprise the opposition to all oppressions, discriminations and domination perpetrated within consumer society, including the abuse of the earth, which is of course perpetuated by continued consumerism. Certain green, feminist and peace movements may be particularly appropriate vehicles for challenging complacent consumer society in the name of a 'conserver' society, or with forms of critique that distinguish between consumption (proper, and pleasurable, use of commodities) and consumerism (lifestyles geared to possession and acquisition).[59] There are indeed limits to satisfaction. Social theory has to acknowledge the centrality of consumption and consumerism if it is have anything relevant to say to the (post)modern world.[60]

And not only theory. Ethically and politically, the same issues confront us. Postmodern populism seems inherently democratizing as it demolishes hierarchy and elite. Yet its limitations are also glaring. Market-led democracy is another deception. More hopeful are instances where practical action has accompanied critique, where the voices of the marginalized have been heard through concrete achievements. For instance, in some urban contexts – such as Vancouver – rejection of post-war modernist housing theory has stimulated the development of housing co-ops which express difference while reducing dependency.[61]

One concept likely to grow in significance is 'citizenship'. Even though it too can easily be coopted by the market, attempts are multiplying to derive a postmodern politics from a revised and revived notion of social participation as citizenship.[62] Attractive to many feminists, rightly critical of male notions of sameness, citizenship also deserves a hearing in Bauman's consumer world of the seduced and the repressed. Why should those unable or unwilling to consume – on a societal or global level – be excluded from full participation in social life? Citizenship could also be a mobilizing

concept in opposition to the new social management involving con-
sumer-citizen electronic surveillance.[63] Though Bauman thinks
panoptic methods are reserved for the repressed, consumer desires
are also channelled and conditioned, and consumers produced, by
methods owing much to quasi-panoptic principles.[64]

If postmodernity means anything, it means the consumer society.
If this position is correct, much has indeed changed, and it seems
to add up to an unprecedented social condition. Indeed, even consumer *society* is a misnomer, unless by it we refer to something well
beyond the conventional bounds of the nation state. Consumerism
is global, not in the sense that all may consume, but in the sense
that all are affected by it. But unless we are content to celebrate
consumerism, wish to wallow in wealth creation, or sink ourselves
in simulacra, the search is still on for an ethical edge, a critical
handle on postmodernity.

Difference and heterogeneity are all very well, but must everyone 'face up to' the idea that there is nothing more? If so, the postmodern really is morally, socially and spiritually bankrupt. Against
that, Mike Featherstone hints at seeking a 'commonality [that]
entails the capacity to recognize differences as legitimate and valid
. . . a common culture' based at a deep cultural level in a common
language.[65] This seems to go beyond both McLuhan's secular Pen-
tecost of the 'global village' and Vattimo's emancipatory Babel.
Others may think on similar lines of 'solidarity with sufferers',
'compassion and neighbour-love', or 'citizenship'.[66] The lines of
contention are likely to converge at this point. Contemporary com-
munitarianism tries to revive commonality but often seems to rein-
state hierarchy or to resist individualism in ways that deny
individuality. Nonetheless, some communitarians do point to actual
practices grounded in forms of life, and in real suffering, which, as
Scott Lash notes, may yield some common language between them
and postmodern ethicists.[67]

Those theorists of postmodernity whose work will survive, I
suspect, are those who stress the ethical seriousness of postmodern
conditions. The playfulness has passed of 'anything goes'. But as
the mask of illusions is torn off in the self-dismantling stage of modernity – that is, postmodernity – a lot of rethinking remains to be
done.[68] Bauman, for instance, rejects the universality and foundationalism of modern ethics, and yet sees the demand for ethical
behaviour as an inescapable aspect of being human. Following

Emmanuel Lévinas, he says we assume moral responsibility for the other as 'the first reality of the self, a starting point rather than the product of society'.[69] The contrast with consumerism could hardly be more marked. It is not without irony, however, that Lévinas's position echoes an ancient and strong strand of religiously rooted ethics, while Bauman has little at all positive to say about such roots. This despite the latter's focus on figures like the 'stranger', who, along with widows and orphans, were the most concretely vulnerable persons in that ancient world.

But many of these ideas hark back to modern not to mention pre-modern times. Can they possibly be reintegrated with the social and cultural analysis of (post)modern times? Such a move might threaten to undercut the claim that postmodernity is an unprecedented condition. And once on this trail, retracing our steps back through modernity, all manner of phenomena could reappear in new light. Already, the prehistory of consumerism is being researched. Colin Campbell's *The Romantic Ethic and the Spirit of Modern Consumerism*[70] shows how the popular view that 'romantic' advertising is put to work to promote producers' interests can be switched round. Romanticism – which, like the 'Protestant ethic', itself derived in part from religious sources – played a part in the very genesis of today's consumerism.

It seems like a case of 'new directions, old dilemmas'. Things to come are not necessarily shapeless; the socio-logic of consumerist postmodernity seems sound, even though consumer culture is fluid, fissiparous. But the new makes us view the old in fresh light. And we find that what seemed novel and unprecedented, actually is fore-shadowed in the old. This need not detract from the stark and raw freshness of contemporary social conditions, or their unique challenge. But it does activate warning signs, that caution against accepting a wholesale shift to the new. It is as misguided to assume a complete break between modernity and postmodernity as it was to assume total discontinuity between traditional and modern societies. And what is sauce for the social goose is sauce for the cultural gander.

Postmodernity, *Fin de Millénaire* and the Future

'Well. It wasn't an excursion. It was the end of the world.'
Timothy Findley, *Not Wanted on the Voyage*[1]

The question of postmodernity is now central to any attempt to chart cultural change and, if this book is correct, to understand contemporary social phenomena. This does not mean that some fully-fledged new society has been born or that, if such a thing could be identified, it would be best to call it postmodern. Wolfgang Welsch fence-sits, appropriately, with 'our postmodern modernity'.[2] For the question of postmodernity offers an opportunity to reappraise modernity, to read the signs of the times as indicators that modernity itself is unstable, unpredictable, and seems to forsake the foreclosed future that it once seemed to promise.

The lines of the preceding argument run as follows. The sense of fragmentation and uncertainty seen in today's art and architecture, movies and music, creates a new cultural collage, a *mélange* of styles and products that collapse into each other in kaleidoscopic confusion. But while the new luminaries – first the French, but now also from many other parts of the world – have achieved fame and notoriety for their analyses of this image-centred, hyperreal world emerging from the ruins of the Enlightenment's grand narratives, these themes are actually prefigured in the work of earlier European thinkers such as Simmel, Nietzsche and Heidegger. What they noted has often been neglected within sociology, too often obsessed with its relation to the natural sciences, with the result that only now is sociology-in-general waking up to the significance of culture.[3] The culture of postmodernism is taken to be evidence of linked social shifts, referred to as postmodernity.

To comprehend the deepest current of change it is helpful to see how not only the Enlightenment, but before that the Reformation tore holes in the unified cultural cosmos of the west. Having once split the symbolic canopy of medievalism, the way was opened for further fragmentation. What Karl Marx noted as a feature of capitalism's corrosive effects can be generalized in regard to modernity: the dismantling of venerable tradition, the restless search for new ways of doing things, produces constant change. So modernity's triumphs – economic growth, urbanism, democratic polity, technoscience, globalism – turn out to be two-edged. From nineteenth-century Romantic reactions to twentieth-century postmodernism, questions are raised about the desirability and utility of the modern legacy. One outcome is Nihilism, with its many faces; helplessness, complacency, *jouissance*, ethical questing and so on. Once, Providence was doubted as a means of interpreting history, but now Progress, its secular counterpart, succumbs to the same fate. Modernity is going nowhere. On this account, we are in a *post*modern condition.

Following the consumer boom after the Second World War, great hopes were vested in the possibilities of postindustrial society which would both place behind us the inequities of earlier capitalism and foster a new social condition based on knowledge. Computers and telecommunications were central to this vision. But as the postindustrial was transposed into postmodern key, progress evaporated, leaving only the as yet little understood iconocentric and cybernetic world of data-processing, mass electronic surveillance, globalized networks and virtual realities. Increasingly, technique takes over. In health, welfare, education and politics, as well as in industry, managerialism reigns. Questions of purposes in education, life and death in medicine, and social goals in politics are reduced to performance criteria; 'Can we manage?' is the main question.

Where does this leave us? It all depends who is the 'us'. Postmodernism is the new but paradoxical cultural paradigm. Is this a liberated carnival to celebrate or the self-seeking narcissism one might expect of the Enlightenment's autonomous self? The demise

of colonialism and rise of new media may make room for suppressed voices to be heard, but why should we listen to one voice
any more than another? The dazzling displays of the shopping malls
and TV ads may seem to offer a consumer cornucopia, but shall
'we' henceforth discover our identity and integration in the marketplace alone? The postmodern: an excursion? The end of the world?
Or something else?

Positioning the postmodern

These paradoxes push us again to the question: what kind of
phenomenon is the postmodern? It is easy to brush it off im-
patiently as intellectual fad and fashion but this would fly in the face
of some significant evidence for seismic social-cultural shifts. One
way to approach the problem is to explore the postmodern as an
experience of crisis, comparing and contrasting it with other such
periods to discover what resolutions, if any, were sought before. We
have seen how Bruno was right to see *Blade Runner* as posing historical questions, which have not gone away despite the postmodern preoccupation with space. By situating postmodern
phenomena in time, we might be able to discern what sorts of questions – of knowing and being, of ethics and politics – are raised, and
also to understand better why the postmodern might be seen as a
moment of death or life, of withering or flowering, of cynical resignation or realistic hope.

One possible parallel with the current crisis of modernity is the
Baroque crisis of the first half of the seventeenth century. As Bryan
Turner says:

> Like our own time, the Baroque crisis, especially in Spain and France,
> was sparked off by unmanageable fiscal crises resulting from a trans-
> formation of the world economy, and it was associated with a chronic
> urban crisis of population growth and urban unrest. More importantly,
> Baroque politics were a response to the cultural crisis of the Protestant
> Reformation, and its associated individualism and commercialism.[4]

This period produced Liebniz's theodicy, justifying this as the best
of all worlds, Monteverdi's music as sound-alchemy, Bernini's
sculptures divinizing sexuality and so on. High and low culture were
mixed, a fascination developed with the artificial and contrived,
together with an interest in metaphor and melancholy. Behind this

an absolutist state attempted to reintegrate its subjects through the production of a kind of mass culture. Of course, such analogies are limited, but the coming of modernity has certainly not erased all tendencies to political authoritarianism or succeeded in protecting people from the vagaries of the market.

Another parallel might be made with *fin de siècle* turbulence a century ago, or even with millennialism. Emile Durkheim's work on suicide and the division of labour, and Sigmund Freud's on aggression, were explicitly connected with the uneasiness, anxiety, disenchantment and malaise they discerned within modern civilization. The heartless and bloodless Enlightenment modernity led to a search for antidotes in the 'irrationalities' (Durkheim) or the 'illusion' (Freud) of religion.[5] It is interesting, to say the least, in the light of this to note the growth of 'New Age' religious manifestations accompanying the growth of other postmodern phenomena since the 1980s.[6] But not only New Age: discussions of postmodernity have also spawned scepticism about secularity in general. Religion is back on the sociological agenda.[7]

Towards the end of the first millennium, Barry Smart reminds us, 'Western civilization was beset by fears about the end of the world, the eruption of "legions of the devil" out of the East, and the prospect that epidemics would wipe out humankind.'[8] So we should not be taken in too easily by talk of totally new times! But it is true that today hope is in short supply, since the postmodern future is turned in on itself, rather as *Blade Runner* portrays it. Susan Sontag says: 'the look into the future, which was once tied to a vision of linear progress, with more knowledge at our disposal than anyone could have dreamed, turned into a vision of disaster'.[9] But as Martin Jay observes, several postmodern theorists indulge in dire fantasies of 'apocalypse forever', which pick up only the first motif from the two normally evoked by religious apocalypse, destruction *and* revelation.[10] Ecological disaster, moral panic in the wake of AIDS, these represent the abyss beyond which, for Baudrillard and his Canadian exponent Arthur Kroker at least, no redemptive moment lies.[11]

A backward glance at apparent parallels serves to relativize our own perceived crises. One might hope that recalling how fears for the second millennium were not realized might help curb the apocalypticism evident in some postmodern accounts. On the other hand, attending to the nature of contemporary 'crises' may also help us recognize what is going on. What in premodern societies were 'dangers' related to stormy weather, crop failure or disease have in the modern world been augmented by 'risks' created by the very processes of modernity we have been examining – ecological and nuclear risks being only the most obvious.[12] Surely there must be ways of facing such risks without succumbing either to the hollow optimism of modern progressivism or to the shrug of permanent postmodern apocalypse?

Maybe, but many writers note that the turn of the twentieth century is the close of the second *Christian* millennium. Manuel Castells opens his trilogy on 'The Information Age' by observing that the millennial shift of the 'Christian era' coincides with major technological and social changes, seen in networking and globalization, against which religious commitment appears as defensive reaction. Others imply that some sources of present crises may be traced to that religious heritage, so that any hope still vested there is misplaced. As we have seen, the arguments for the partial rooting of modernity in Christian soil are strong, in terms of the origins both of capitalism *and* of technoscience. It comes as no surprise, then, given the connections between technoscience and (post)modern discourses, that technology critics such as David Noble (in *The Religion of Technology*) and Donna Haraway (in *Modest_Witness@Second_Millennium*) make these points.[13]

Haraway sees 'Christian realism' at the heart of American technoscience, especially in its genetic and information sciences, a 'millennarian discourse about beginnings and ends, first and last things, suffering and progress, figure and fulfillment'. The Oncomouse on the back cover 'doesn't have a crown of thorns on her head for no reason'.[14] The millennial moment, for Haraway, should be grasped by those heretics, infidels and Jews wishing to 'reprogram the time machine' in the 'interests of a deeper, broader, and more open scientific literacy' than that which has in her view overwhelmingly informed modern technoscience thus far. But while some Christianity-and-technoscience connections may be stiflingly narrow, surely exploration of cyborg potential is not the only alternative way forward. Within the 'diffraction' process commended by Haraway it would be surprising to find that the religious motifs that helped 'make a difference' in the first place had all been so drained of their power as to render them incapable of repeating the performance.

The nagging question remains: if postmodernity means the exhaustion of modernity, or at least draws our attention to modernity's limits, what now is an appropriate stance towards modernity? This question is made doubly difficult by the Janus-faced character of postmodernity, seen above in the discussions of science, consumption and the body. Has modernity reached a terminal point so that, even if resuscitation attempts were made, they would be futile? Does modernity yet possess a flicker of life that might be fanned back to flame, or is it actually much more robust than this? Is there any other way of handling its current condition? In what follows, three responses are outlined: accepting the postmodern; reasserting of the modern; and reclaiming the premodern. They do not necessarily exclude each other.

Redefining reality

The postmodern condition is integrally yoked with consumer capitalism. Contemporary postmodern queries began in the realms of art and architecture, TV, taste and style, and these phenomena have continued to dominate debate. Modern sociology, having established itself on the idea that the 'social' is a special sphere in its own right, now reels from the reminder that cultural forces are always mixed up with the social. Despite Max Weber's focus on the spirit and ethos of capitalism, or even Karl Marx's on commodity fetishism, most sociology has chosen to pursue questions of capitalism as productive relations involving labourers, managers and so on.[15] Today's postmodern challenge returns the spotlight to the ideals, values and symbols of economic life, as they appear in the lives of consumers and in consumerism. Taste and style, far from being marginal reflexes of production, are now viewed as centrally significant.

The very items that modernity used to banish ambivalence and uncertainty, techniques such as managerialism or science and technology, now help to undermine the modern sense of reality. Modern mass technologies of communication, for instance, allow for great expansion of services and leisure industries and for mushrooming simulations of reality. This is especially true for Baudrillard, who announces, 'TV is the world.' Consumer lifestyles and tastes are supported by such media, with complex consequences. Clothing – or rather the Benetton or Levi labels – can simultaneously serve to distinguish social statuses, thus giving a sense of identity and social integration to the wearer, *and* offer the chance to feel comfortable with what will 'please yourself'.[16] The body itself may be pierced, remodelled, reshaped, and perhaps even cloned for consumption, the last possibility being a challenge to chosen identities if ever there was one!

Not only this, but the very idea of meaning becomes questionable. For meaning to mean anything, some stable boundaries, fixed structures, shared consensus are assumed. But in a media-dominated world, meaning dissolves.[17] Anything goes, or so it seems. The old distinctions between high and mass culture are rendered vacuous by their prodigal juxtaposition in the TV and other media. Radio programmes mix folk, rock and classical music, loosening or moving the boundaries between them. But even these categories appear somewhat sclerotic. Music becomes far more liquescent as styles spill promiscuously over the lips of their conventional containers, from funk to fusion or from rave to rap. The erstwhile guardians of taste and expert opinion shudder to watch their neat hierarchies tumble before their eyes like so many children's building blocks. Intellectuals, once used to a 'legislative' role that handed down judgements from an elevated position, now redefine their task as 'interpreting' between groups playing different language games. The seminar supplants the lecture.[18]

Such redefining of reality can be seen in two ways. The idea of 'one history' that unifies the world is scarcely tenable any more. The sense of space in the global, that flattens old hierarchies and reveals the many different histories of local peoples, also discloses difference and a need to find fresh modes of communication. More negatively, it may be felt that postmodern corrosives eat away at the foundations of grand schemes of the Enlightenment, the expansive spread of westernization, and the optimistic dreams that made modernity bearable if not enjoyable. All lie exposed as fictions, the super-stories of progress. As Lyotard says, they are no longer believable; 'incredulity towards metanarratives' is the order of the day. But they are not only fictions; power is involved. Foucault's studies of the modern 'discourses' on penal practices, sexuality and psychology suggest that their supposed 'rationality' is pretence. According to him, such discourses produce the very subjects that modern social sciences thought were their irreducible agents.

Needless to say, the ghost of Nietzsche hovers around these

accounts. For Foucault, as for Nietzsche, the will to power is bound up with establishing any truth. Nietzsche's achievement lay in revealing the false pretensions of moral philosophy. His 'genealogical unmasking' informs a profoundly sceptical postmodernism. There was no progress of rational thought in the nineteenth century. 'God is dead', proclaimed Nietzsche, meaning that foundational thought has been dissolved. We each just belong to our own historical tradition.[19] But this is not an occasion for mourning or for bemoaning decadence. Rather, the possibilities of an honest and realistic appraisal of our situation now open before us.

Despite the despair and angst of some, one wing of postmodernism exudes a sense of *jouissance*, of celebration. This might be understood as escaping the shackles of modernist assumptions and expectations, such that postmodernists relax in a playground of irony and irreverent pastiche, where pluralism and difference contrast with the older 'terrorism' of totalizing discourses. 'Here's to heterogeneity!' might be its slogan.[20] As David Harvey remarks, 'Postmodernism swims, even wallows, in the fragmentary and chaotic currents of change as if that's all there is.'[21] But if ecstasy, enthusiasm and even emancipation are promised in the postmodern, it may also be purposeful. For Helène Cixous, a delicious *double entendre* occurs in *jouissance*, sounds that could also be spelled, *j'ouis sens* – 'I detect meaning'. Feminine pleasure, enjoyment, may be counter-hegemonic in the serious sense that human fulfilment is no longer restricted to male definition.

The world of TV both is part of, and helps to, drive consumer culture. On the networks, though not necessarily on cable TV, concern with surfaces is central; there is nothing 'behind' the rapid movement of successive images. Indeed, the supposed penchant for remotely controlled channel-hopping has become an archetypical image of the postmodern. The idea that there might be depth is alien to the 'true' postmodern: it is just such essential meanings and substructural phenomena that postmodernism denies and derides. So Umberto Eco can claim Disneyland as America's Sistine Chapel,[22] and Baudrillard can say that Disneyland is presented as imaginary to make us believe that the rest of America is real. With Disneyland as the symbolic American utopia,[23] even history transforms itself to consumer demands in the late-twentieth-century craze for museums and heritage parks.

While many self-styled postmoderns may accept, and embrace,

seeming chaos, others find in postmodern circumstances a challenge to rethink, redefine reality. Foucault advises us to 'prefer what is positive and multiple, difference over uniformity, flows over unities, mobile arrangements over systems'.[24] Foucault hinted that the way forward is via the new social movements spawned by the 1960s – feminists, gays and so on. 'Heterotopia', where apparently incongruous worlds coexist, is our situation. Lyotard's insight about our involvement in different linguistics registers is that we are all engaged in our own local games, which we play differently depending on where we are – office, church, sportsfield, pub. What we know, he suggests, is only valid locally. If some institutions still try to impose on us their definition of reality, ways exist of challenging them. For Lyotard, an appropriate strategy would be to 'open the databanks' to all. But who would know what to do with the infoglut? We would virtually drown in the flood. There must be another way.

Vattimo, for whom postmodernity is the society of generalized communication, of mass media, sees 'transparency' as the key.[25] The end of colonialism, freeing ethnic voices, and the emergence of mass media, stimulating cultural relativity, has created an irreversibly pluralist situation. The old realities, the world of objects measured and manipulated by technoscience, are lost. But the loss is no cause for regret. Rather, a new ideal of emancipation emerges, 'based on oscillation, plurality and, ultimately, on the erosion of the very "principle of reality"'.[26] Babel is valued; disorientation becomes a virtue. Nietzsche's *Übermensch*, the 'beyond-man' comes into his own at last. No more nostalgia for the fixed, stable and permanent. The postmodern experience of oscillation is an 'opportunity of a new way of being (finally, perhaps) human'.[27]

Of course, these proposals provoke many responses. The one thought I wish to insert here concerns what might be missing from these intimations of, and invitations to, postmodernity. Is the chaos as complete as it seems? Are all foundations totally absent? Though the reality principle may be questioned, can it really be avoided (think of *Lawnmower Man*)? Do these postmodern thinkers really manage without metanarratives? Are their ideas really no more than Gilles Deleuze's 'projectiles launched into time'? It seems strange, for instance, that Richard Rorty pulls back from pragmatism when dealing with opponents. Instead of asking if it is good for us to believe this or that[28] he just pinpoints the errors

of his opponents. As we shall see in a moment, Habermas charge
Foucault with 'performative contradiction' for surreptitiously using
the tools of reason. Likewise Lyotard, whose notion of postmodernity seems to be supported by another metanarrative (a residual
Marxism?); Kellner suggests there can be no theory without one.[29]
Perhaps in the end even Baudrillard has a 'submerged religious
paradigm'. His work on *America* can be read as a moral pilgrimage.
He dismisses the bad nostalgia of Europe but finds only shallow-
ness and superficiality in the New World.

What is to be made of this? Clearly, western ways, that is, European and North American cultures, can no longer be seen as normative, paradigmatic. But does this mean we cheerfully consign the
whole western tradition to the garbage bag of history without any
regrets? I think not. Equally clearly, the emergence of peoples and
cultures hitherto hidden in the shadow of western imperialism is to
be welcomed. Westerners are right, it seems to me, to try and hear
at last the voices of those too long victimized by ethnic, religious
and gender oppression. The very term 'Orientalism' has been a
means, argues Edward Said, of creating a subordinate 'other'.[30]
However hard it is to resist the postmodern pressure to define ourselves in terms of difference, the only real hope for true toleration
must lie in discovering what 'we' have in common as well as in
respecting diversity.

Many of those engaged in post-colonial studies in the past decade
are attracted to the field because of personal experience. Thus, for
instance, Madan Sarup, an ethnic Indian raised in Bristol, England,
was shocked to hear a colleague at dinner describe his home as a
'white man's house'. She sparked a sea change in his – until then,
Marxist – thinking, to such an extent that his last book pursued the
themes of the meaning of home, the journey of the migrant, and the
crossing of the border.[31] When such an autobiographical start is
made, several stages follow. For example, it is inadequate merely
to recognize how subordinate others are created, and then to settle
for suspension of judgement on the 'weak pluralist' assumption that
everything about the other culture is equally valuable. As Satya
Mohanty argues, real disagreements and cultural clashes must be
confronted, and not merely ignored as unresolvable, if genuine
respect and understanding are to result. 'Difficult epistemic and
ethical negotiations' are their prelude.[32]

This also has consequence for considering contemporary 'victims'.

▀hould we accept as eagerly each and every self-proclaimed victim Ɔf time and circumstance? Are there no limits to who may legitimately claim victim status? Again, mere diversity and disorientation will not do as guides to the pressing issues of either fairly adjudicating such claims, or the broader ones mentioned above, of human-made risks. Without some alternative vision, it is hard to see how some postmodern stances will not degenerate into mere complacency or self-seeking cynicism. Pleas for properly ethical approaches, such as Mohanty's, are a welcome outcome of post-colonial debates. The challenge of (post)modern conditions is to seek new forms of critical theory that both avoid moralism and provide adequate protections for those – such as the poor – whose vulnerability to exploitation and domination is greatest.

Accepting chaos, welcoming Babel, these may be ways of undermining and subverting modernity's *hubris*. As Kroker says, with characteristic energy, 'Here, finally, is a theoretical vocabulary and a language of decolonization for piercing the closed horizon of technology, and for listening intently to the "intimations of deprival" in the midst of the celebratory ruins of the American way.'[33] What this prompts, however, is an earnest ethical turn within postmodern discourse. For while many have assumed, not without justification, that the postmodern leads from Nietzsche, 'beyond good and evil', in fact ethical concerns are increasingly expressed by leading postmodern theorists.[34] From the mid-1980s on, this has provided a rationale for investigating possible links between postmodern and critical theory.[35]

Persisting with modernity

If postmodernity catalyses a reappraisal of modernity, it must be said that some conclude that modernity looks inviting compared with what they see as the postmodern step beyond all boundaries. If all the postmodern can offer is randomness and chaos, play and pastiche, consumerism and unconcern, such critics might conclude that modernity held some attractions. And if the postmodern condition appears unable to support itself without at least implicit reference to motifs more properly found in paradigms denied by postmoderns, then something is awry in postmodernism.

Of course, some scorn the whole project and cast their vote for a full-blooded return to Enlightenment rationalism. It may not be emotionally satisfying, admits Ernest Gellner, but as a way of obtaining knowledge and determining morality, it is still our best hope.[36] But our present concern is more with those who accept some of the force of the postmodern critique while denying that our cultural and social condition is beyond or after modernity. That is, modernity may well be in trouble, but the crises are resolvable still within a modernist frame. Some potentials of modernity are as yet unrealized, perhaps even untested. Modernity may be faltering, or altering its shape dramatically, but as yet insufficient evidence has emerged to say our condition is postmodern.

The best known critic of the postmodern among social theorists is Jürgen Habermas. It has been said that Habermas's entire project is a *new* Dialectic of Enlightenment, which both sees and explains the dark side of the Enlightenment legacy and still redeems and justifies the hope of freedom, justice and happiness.[37] He fears that the postmodern mood represents a turning away from both political responsibilities and a concern for suffering (even though it is hard to square this with, for instance, the post-colonialist positions alluded to above). Habermas attacks today's intellectuals for 'returning (via Derrida and Heidegger) to Nietzsche, searching for salvation in the portentious moods of the cultic rejuvenation of a young conservatism'.[38] Perhaps this 'neoconservatism and aesthetically-inspired anarchism, in the name of a farewell to modernity, are merely trying to revolt against it once again'.[39]

For Habermas, as we saw earlier, modernity is simply an incomplete project. Along with others he questions the foundationalist approaches to science, but denies that this precludes any kind of social science. Again, with others he notes the significance of new technologies of communication, but doubts that computers and TVs make a qualitative difference to our cultural experience, any more than telegraphs and telephones did. Similar conclusions are reached by Anthony Giddens, who acknowledges the radicalizing of Enlightenment scepticism as 'high' but definitely not as 'post' modern.[40] He too attacks the pretended objectivity of social science, but insists that a hermeneutic approach can still yield realistic accounts of the social.

So where lies the way forward for the modern project? Habermas still finds promise in what he calls 'communicative rationality'. Barriers to free and open communication must be dismantled, with the goal in mind of an 'ideal speech situation'. In the modern period, the ocial system – the bureaucracy, capitalism – has increasingly encroached on the 'life-world', that sphere of active subjects trying to understand each other. Rationalization has occurred in the system at the expense of the life-world, so the two require re-coupling. The way forward, then, is through an expansion of the 'public sphere', a process already encouraged by the growth of new social movements that resist further life-world colonization.

All this is too much for Foucault, for whom Habermas is a naive utopian. By eschewing the idea that any standpoint, any universal principle exists by which our situation may be judged, Foucault believes he undercuts Habermas's critical theory. But Habermas counters this by arguing that Foucault himself is caught in the paradox of performative contradiction: he cannot but use the reason he so badly wishes to overthrow. Others, too, have noted Foucault's smuggling of critical claims and epistemic standpoints into his work, without ever acknowledging or explaining them.[41] Derrida, on the other hand, freely acknowledges that his project necessitates using the very tools that he criticizes. For Habermas, naturally, this is further evidence that modernity cannot be so easily shaken off. Another possibility is that they simply talk past each other, drawing on different understandings of 'reason'.

The desire to ground critical theory in some specific standpoint also holds others back from full acceptance of postmodern agendas, even though they may be intrigued or persuaded by some of their features. While some Marxists are unashamedly derisive about postmodernity – Alex Callinicos, for instance – others, such as the literary critic Fredric Jameson or social geographer David Harvey have made extensive and erudite studies of the phenomenon. Jameson makes his own position quite clear: postmodernism is late capitalism's cultural logic.[42] It represents a break in the system, away from both earlier market and imperial stages which, though technically possible after the Second World War, is culturally more recent. Within what might also be termed the 'image or spectacle society', mass culture has eroded the distinction between the real and the imaginary, but not to the point of complete obliteration. The capitalist totality remains the starting point for critique, very much in the spirit of Theodor Adorno's neo-Marxism.

Analogous moves are made by some feminists. While many feminists might welcome the dismantling of hierarchy and the de-privileging of patriarchal voices in modernity, they still do not wish

to lose sight of alternative social realities that would serve ⸱
ground their analyses and critique. Situated knowledge(s), posi-
tional standpoints, critical stances – these all suggest that the search
for a centre, for some criteria of judgement, for something to unify
and make sense of the fragmented and the fluid, persists in social
theory, and not just in its nostalgic or reactionary varieties. Linda
Nicholson, for example, shows that, at face value, feminism and
postmodernism seem to be natural allies. Both question the 'God's-
eye view' quest for scientific knowledge secularized by the
Enlightenment into a search for universal principles to lay bare the
features of natural and social reality.[43] Such 'objectivity' and 'neu-
trality' were vulnerable to attack as cloaks for biased and partial
accounts. The reality, she claims, is that all 'findings' of social
science are limited by their local and historical location. However,
fresh dangers lurk nearby. Relativism and the abandonment of
theory bode ill for a politically charged analytical enterprise like
feminism. Much feminism stops short of full embrace of the postmodern, making limited claims for cumulative science or non-total-
izing theory.

Without invoking either Marxism or feminism, social philosopher Charles Taylor probably speaks for many when he too tries to
defend aspects of the Enlightenment legacy.[44] Candidly acknowledging what he calls the 'malaise of modernity', he nonetheless still
finds in modernity glimmers of light. Without wishing to be counted
among either modernity's 'boosters' or its 'knockers', Taylor says
that the modern ideal of authenticity represents a way forward. Far
from the narcissistic self-absorption imputed to it by its detractors,
authenticity, being true to self and others, and accepting the force
of moral claims beyond the satisfaction of self, offers a cure to
modernity's complex malaise.

Lastly, mention should be made of those sociologists – not
necessarily Marxists, feminists or liberals – who propose that we
accept the idea of postmoder*nity* without relapsing into postmoder*nism*. The question is sometimes asked whether a postmodern sociology or a sociology of the postmodern is called for.
Although a 'postmodern sociology' sounds like an oxymoron, given
that discipline's early ambitions to be a (natural) science of society,
writers such as Ann Game have shown how certain methods, such
as deconstruction, may produce fresh forms of theorizing. In
Undoing the Social she proposes that sociology be read as fiction;

is not a 'transparent medium for representing the social or the real'.[45] Instead of the 'authoritarian address' of much sociology, she seeks to 'know with her body' – stressing the immediacy of the temporal, of ordinary, everyday experiences. As we have seen, adequate responses to such emphases will increasingly be expected of sociologies of the present.

But it is not clear that, on their own, deconstructionist (or other 'postmodern') sociologies could replace forms of analysis and theory that attempt to paint with big brushstrokes on a broad canvas. Concern with the past and the future as well as the present calls for more than analyses of memory, significant though such concerns undoubtedly are. As Keith Tester says, 'post-modernity, and the post-modern condition, can only be understood dialectally and in terms of all those modern things which it attempts reflexively to deconstruct and overcome'.[46] Without seeking an explicitly postmodern sociology, then, a number of sociologists have taken up the gauntlet of analysing sociologically the postmodern condition. That is, while being sensitive to properly postmodern questions, but without forsaking the modes of systematic inquiry characteristic of much modern social science, such sociology takes up a fresh agenda around the concept of postmodernity.

Two prominent figures in this regard are Zygmunt Bauman and Mike Featherstone, each of whom focuses on consumers and consumerism. Featherstone's work tries not only to locate the cultural movement of postmodernism, but to investigate how far it portends 'broader cultural shifts in everyday experiences and practices'.[47] Shopping centres are a key example, illustrating the ways that the old calculative rationality no longer underlies these economic transactions. Rather, shopping has become a leisure-time cultural activity, an experience of spectacle, luxury or nostalgia. As cities and local economies are geared to promoting such experiences, are we witness to the emergence of postmodernity? Featherstone's answer would be: it depends. Careful sociological analysis of very conventional kinds would be necessary before any definitive conclusion could be reached.

Bauman, on the other hand, believes we can indeed perceive 'intimations of postmodernity'.[48] Rather than these being a diseased or degenerate form of modernity – or even Taylor's 'malaise' – they add up to a new social reality in their own right. The central character of this sociological story is no longer the worker of

modern times, but instead the consumer. Consumer condu~
becomes the cognitive and moral focus of life – consuming is ~
pleasurable duty – the way in which people are integrated into
society, and also the nexus of systemic management. In all this,
however, Bauman does not lose sight of the emancipatory thrust of
critical social theory, nor does he call for new procedures or purposes of sociological work. It is a new object of investigation – postmodernity – that he has in mind.[49]

Both Featherstone and Bauman also comment on globalization, a
process increasingly central to the analysis of postmodernity. Facilitated by media of electronic information and communication, the
globalization of contemporary social life touches on most of the
major issues touched on in this book, from world markets for consumer goods to the demise of the western way of Enlightenment. As
we saw, globalization has little to do with utopian ideas of a 'global
village' or dreams of computerized version of H. G. Wells's 'world
brain', and much more with the way that we are all affected by – and
affect – distant events and processes. Thus Ulrich Beck's concept of
'risk' is inherently global, referring to the ways that oil spills, nuclear
fallout and ozone depletion respect no 'nation state' boundaries.

Within the ranks of sociologists one can find both disagreement
about whether our social condition is 'postmodernity', or 'high',
'late', 'radicalized' or 'reflexive' modernity, and much agreement
on what are the crucial analytical issues for sociology on the eve of
the third millennium. Globalization is one such; and a desire to discover a new ethics, a new mode of critique, is another. Paradoxically, the search for appropriate ways of living *beyond* modernity
seems to have stimulated a reconsideration of positions stretching
well back *before* modernity.

Reclaiming the premodern

Alasdair MacIntyre's *After Virtue* appeals to a premodern position
following the failure of the Enlightenment project. In a famous pas-
sage he offers the stark alternatives:

> *Either* one must follow through the aspirations and the collapse of the
> different versions of the Enlightenment project until there remains
> only the Nietzschean diagnosis and the Nietzschean problematic *or*
> one must hold that the Enlightenment project was not only mistaken,

ɔut should never have been commenced in the first place. There is no third alternative.[50]

The choice lies between Nietzsche and Aristotle, between no morality and morality. In the polity based on virtue we have to accept that there exists a 'right' and 'natural' way for human beings which is grasped by looking above or beyond those humans. The education of citizens in the virtues is of central importance, because this inculcates the desirable goals.

In MacIntyre's view, medievalism should never have been broken up by the Reformation because this movement simply boosted the fragmentation then wrought by modernity. The way forward, then as now, would be to pursue the rational quest for a social tradition in which the Aristotelian moral and political texts are canonical. Others have claimed that MacIntyre actually depends more than he knows on the traditions of modernity that he rejects[51] – his position is close to that of Charles Taylor, for instance, who draws on Aristotle and Augustine but sees himself as a modern[52] – but the point is made: modernity is a mistake; Aristotle is the antidote.

Interestingly enough, some postmodern thinkers also consider possibilities from the premodern. Lyotard, for instance, thinks we are 'in the position of Aristotle's prudent individual, who makes judgements about the just and the unjust without the least criterion'.[53] Foucault and Derrida, for all their disaccord, could be said to agree in the end on ethics, deriving from the Greeks. In Foucault, this might be the imperative for 'self-discipline', although as Roy Boyne observes, 'the resources of the *logos* are needed to give shape and direction to this power'.[54] Lyotard, Derrida and others often refer to the Jewish philosopher Emmanuel Levinas,[55] who insists that there can never be a theoretical justification for ethics. They always come from outside, from the voice of the Other. Of course, Lyotard stresses that our present condition is one of pluralist paganism and therefore he sidesteps the logic of Levinas's position, obeying the voice of Yahweh. But it is nonetheless not insignificant that such postmodern ethical comment harks back to the premodern.

A similar anti-Enlightenment offensive to MacIntyre's may be found in the work of Canadian George Grant, or, more recently, in that of the British social theologian John Milbank. Grant harks back to Platonic and Christian sources, while for Milbank, Augustine rather than Aristotle has pride of place. Grant saw Nietzsche as the great architect of modernity, who taught that humanity has to make its own history without the aid of God or a natural order. Modern technology expressed this Nietzschean spirit, for Grant, and thus it was virtually unassailable. Grant tried to mobilize a Platonic Christianity, in which the suffering God of the cross was central, against Nietzsche and technology. So far from Christianity being hopeless servility (as it was for Nietzsche), it was the very ground of hope.[56] One would have to go beyond Grant, of course, to discover ways in which that hope could extend to today's technoscience, but the essential clue is there. Alternatives are available to idolized technology.

Milbank also maintains that what he calls secular reason, though damaging enough in its Enlightenment forms, finds its most virulent manifestation in Nietzschean nihilism. For him, only the Christian *mythos* is capable of standing against nihilism, so he is unrelenting in his attack on other sub-, a- and anti-Christian options. Violence is present as a result of the desire to dominate, and this can be seen in both modern and postmodern forms. Rather than grounding his critique in 'science' or even 'tradition', however, Milbank points to the Christian hope (as confidence, not optimism) of peace as an alternative to foundationalism. Augustine's *City of God*, with its conflicting antithesis, the earthly city, suggests the character of the ongoing struggle. Faith, and the community of the faithful, is the key to the future. Interestingly enough, Augustine's great work was a response to cultural and political crisis in the crumbling Roman Empire as it retreated into tribalism. His message was that Christians should neither identify themselves with the fortunes of the empire, nor retreat into a defensive ghetto.

Milbank's is a strident and uncompromising position, but one that demands attention for just that reason. Regrettably, he does not integrate an understanding of the gendered dimension of human relationships into his theory of *dominium* and of what I would refer to as *shalom* (the word 'peace' has too many connotations of tranquillity or absence of conflict to do justice to the concept). His work would also benefit from dialogue with other similarly minded people working in parallel traditions.[57] But he does highlight the radicality and vitality of what could be thought of as a 'premodern' position, and its relevance to 'postmodern'

~~iditions.~~ He demonstrates how such a position can be held ~~~~thout relapsing into nostalgia, authoritarianism or fundamental-~~~~sm, thus outflanking potential postmodern parries.

One does not have to join MacIntyre, Grant or Milbank in their final dismissal of the modern to accept the force of their arguments that the premodern still has much to offer in the debate over (post)modernity. Rather than seeing the postmodern as a deviation or the demise of the modern, here the modern itself is portrayed as a mistaken world-view and misguided social order. Ancient wisdom is retrieved as the means of constructive critique that relativizes both modernity and postmodernity. What it would take to convince others of their positions is as yet unclear, although I suspect that more resonance exists between their work and the postmodern 'ethical turn' than they might at first allow. Combined with Latour's insistence that we never were modern, in any complete sense, the door is open for a serious reappraisal of contemporary conditions, one that does not simplistically assume that certain ethical, epistemic or even religious resources are no longer available.

Conclusions

Let me try to sum up in a few paragraphs the main conclusions that can be derived from this brief survey of postmodernity. First, the concept of postmodernity is a valuable 'problematic' that alerts us to key questions concerning contemporary social changes.[58] I see it as a concept that invites participation in a debate over the nature and direction of present-day societies, in a globalized context, rather than one describing an already existing state of affairs. Quite unprecedented social and cultural shifts are occurring; whether or not 'postmodernity' is the best term to sum them up is a moot point. The important thing is to understand what is happening, not to agree on a concept to capture it with. 'Postmodernity' will do fine for now.

Second, the ways that debates over postmodernity are inextricably intertwined with those concerning postmodernism act as a vital reminder that the social and the cultural belong together. Unfortunately, and despite the best efforts in particular of some feminists, much postmodern debate has been conducted in the heady atmosphere of speculative enquiry, without sufficient reference to actual social, economic and political conditions. But equally, much social

analysis has been blind to the cultural dimensions of the po
modern, to the disadvantage of sociology. With respect to info
mation and communication technologies especially, there is an
urgent need for social and cultural analysis to proceed in tandem.
The emerging social order, whether conceived as 'post-' or 'high'
modern, is characterized above all by new modes of communication.

Third, the debate over postmodernity stimulates a reappraisal of
modernity as a social-cultural phenomenon. The most obvious
example we have discussed concerns the relation between work
and consumption. While the occupational structure will continue to
yield important data for understanding the nature of contemporary
information-oriented societies on a global scale, our grasp of the
daily realities and meanings of social life is more likely to be
enhanced by considering consumers, not just workers. As Marx,
Weber and Durkheim showed the connections between the cultural
and religious, and the rise of the industrial worker, so now we need
to understand better the cultural and religious roots – and fruits –
of contemporary consumerism.

Fourth, the postmodern debate forces us to form judgements –
both analytical *and* philosophical – on modernity itself. Did modernity, by secularizing providence into progress, initiate the unrav-
elling of the social-cultural fabric to produce the fragments and
patches that some label nihilism? Can we still work with modernity,
as Habermas or Taylor would counsel, or should we seek to live
beyond it, in Vattimo's disorientation or Baudrillard's asocial
hyperreality? Alternatively, should we rather step back from it, and
see it as an historical era in which, as in others, ancient wisdom from
premodern times still speaks? Each option also brings dilemmas
and demands of its own, but the questions cannot be evaded.

My own sympathies lie in a complex interaction between the premodern, modern and postmodern. I am committed to social analysis of a recognizably sociological – though non-empiricist – kind, but
this leads me to think that some significant shifts are occurring that
fundamentally question the whole edifice of modernity. Yet western
modernity itself was the product of both authentic expressions of
Judeo-Christian[59] culture, *and* would-be autonomous human reason,
so that subsequent generations have been saddled with the typically
modern dualisms of subject–object, thought–action and so forth.
When I align myself with the 'premodern' Christian tradition,

wever, I risk being associated with either reactionary or nostalgic
.ances which in fact I eschew. My critical stance derives from Jesus's
call to love one's neighbour, and an ethic of responsibility,[60] but this
demands that I face up to the implications of a fractured modernity
and today's globalizing, technologized and consumerist social realities.

Last, discussing postmodernity in this broader frame reminds us
that even postmodernity can be contextualized and relativised. I
considered briefly the possibility that the postmodern represents a
fin de millénaire phenomenon, and while this certainly does not
exhaust its possible meanings, living on the cusp of the year 2000
would lead us to expect the flowering of phenomena appropriate to
a new millennium. Millennial hopes and fears seem artificially exaggerated when expressed in a world of high technology and rapid
globalization. The consumerist cornucopia grows symbiotically
with the risk society, creating contradictions that seem starker than
even Marx might have surmised. The postmodern has these contradictions as its backdrop, if not its stimulus. And 'millennial'
movies such as *Blade Runner* provide constructive opportunities to
consider these contradictions in relevant ethical fields from globalism to the body.

Once, the idea that the future is in human hands was confidently
asserted. Thus modern arrogance denied the divine and diverted all
hope to human resources. Today, the human is being displaced,
decentered, and the grip on the future seems once more up for
grabs. While this opens the door to everything from Foucault's play
of power to the Age of Aquarius, it also renders more plausible the
possibility that Providence was not such a bad idea after all.
Perhaps postmodern apocalyptics will have to make space for a
vision of a (re)new(ed) earth, that antique agent of social change,
and the original partner of final judgement. Nietzsche would turn
in his grave.

Notes

Chapter 1

1 See Manuel Castells's trilogy on 'The Information Age', particularly vol. 1, *The Rise of the Network Society* (Oxford and New York: Blackwell, 1996).

2 Giuliana Bruno 'Ramble City: Postmodernism and *Blade Runner*', October, 41, Summer 1987. My comments on the movie are influenced by Bruno and also David Harvey, *The Condition of Postmodernity* (New York: Blackwell, 1990), pp. 308–14; and Gianni Vattimo, *The Transparent Society* (Cambridge: Polity Press, 1992), pp. 83ff.

3 On this, see Hans Jonas, *The Imperative of Responsibility* (New York: Oxford University Press, 1984), but also, Zygmunt Bauman, *Postmodern Ethics* (Oxford and New York: Blackwell, 1993).

Chapter 2

1 Martin Albrow argues this in *The Global Age* (Cambridge: Polity Press, 1996). See especially pp. 78–9.

2 David Bebbington, *Patterns in History* (Leicester: Inter-Varsity Press, 1979), pp. 43ff.

3 This view is expounded by Karl Löwith in *Meaning in History* (Chicago: University of Chicago Press, 1949). Hans Blumenberg denies this thesis in *The Legitimacy of the Modern Age* (Cambridge, MA: MIT Press, 1983), arguing instead that progress 'reoccupied' space left by providence. Modern self-interest can thus be displayed as a 'legitimate' motive of modernity. Blumenberg's scholarship is impressive, but his modification of Löwith's position obscures the fact that progress is an article of faith. See e.g. Bob Goudzwaard, *Capitalism and Progress* (Grand Rapids, MI: Eerdmans, 1979).

Anthony Giddens, *The Consequences of Modernity* (Cambridge: Polity Press, 1990), p. 48.

5 See Zygmunt Bauman, *Modernity and Ambivalence* (Cambridge: Polity Press, 1988).

6 The expression is Bernice Martin's. See her *A Sociology of Contemporary Cultural Change* (Oxford: Blackwell, 1981).

7 See Ernest Gellner *Postmodernism, Reason and Religion* (London and New York: Routledge, 1992), p. 17. Under Khomeini, Islam shifted from Shi'ism towards Sunni 'high' Islam.

8 This distinction is entertained, for instance, by Giddens in *The Consequences of Modernity*, pp. 45–6.

9 Gary Woller (ed.), *Public Administration and Postmodernism*, special issue of *American Behavioral Scientist*, 41:1, 1997, p. 9.

10 Stephen Crook, Jan Pakulski and Malcolm Waters, *Postmodernization: Change in Advanced Society* (London: Sage, 1992).

11 As Mike Featherstone argues, the cultural sphere is not decentred so much as recentred today. At the same time, he insists that social analysis is also required so that cultural particularities be properly understood: 'Yet the extent to which we can all participate in cultural production and consumption clearly varies historically and between societies' (*Undoing Culture: Globalization, Postmodernism, and Identity* (London: Sage, 1995), p. 3).

12 Many understand the relevance of Nietzsche through Gianni Vattimo's *The End of Modernity* (Cambridge: Polity Press) published in this English translation in 1988, 100 years after the original edition of Nietzsche's *The Will to Power*.

13 Jean-François Lyotard, *The Postmodern Condition: A Report on Knowledge* (Minneapolis: University of Minnesota Press, and Manchester: Manchester University Press, 1984), p. 77.

14 Marshall Berman, *All that is Solid Melts into Air* (New York and Harmondsworth: Penguin, 1988), p. 111.

15 William Shakespeare, *The Tempest*, Act 4, Scene 1, l. 150.

16 See C. Stephen Evans, *Passionate Reason: Making Sense of Kierkegaard's Philosophical Fragments* (Bloomington, IN: Indiana University Press, 1992).

17 Gianni Vattimo, *The End of Modernity* (Cambridge: Polity Press, and Baltimore: Johns Hopkins University Press, 1988), p. 4.

18 See the comments of Jon R. Snyder in the translator's introduction to Vattimo's *The End of Modernity*, p. lvi.

19 See below, Chapter 6, p. 131.

20 Zygmunt Bauman, *Intimations of Postmodernity* (London and Boston: Routledge, 1992), p. 31.

21 Quoted in David Frisby, *Fragments of Modernity* (Cambridge MA: MIT Press, 1986), p. 43.

Notes

22 Simmel's best known work is *The Philosophy of Money* (London and Boston: Routledge, 1978).

23 David Frisby, *Simmel and Since* (London and New York: Routledge, 1992), p. 169.

24 The original French edition of Lyotard's book, *La Condition postmoderne: rapport sur le savoir* appeared in 1979 but the English translation was not available until 1984.

25 Lyotard, *The Postmodern Condition*, p. xxiv.

26 Zygmunt Bauman, *Legislators and Interpreters* (Cambridge: Polity Press, 1987).

27 Lyotard, *The Postmodern Condition*, p. 17. The notion of 'language games' comes from Ludwig Wittgenstein who, along with Ferdinand de Saussure, is a tremendously important influence upon postmodern discussions of 'discourse'.

28 Ibid., p. 38.

29 See, for example, Christopher Norris, 'Deconstruction, Postmodernism and Philosophy' in David Wood (ed.), *Derrida: A Critical Reader* (Oxford, UK, and Cambridge, MA: Blackwell, 1992), pp. 167–92.

30 David Harvey, *The Condition of Postmodernity* (Cambridge, MA, and Oxford: Blackwell, 1990), p. 51.

31 Baumann, *Intimations*, p. 133.

32 Luce Irigaray, *Speculum of the Other Woman* (Ithaca, NY: Cornell University Press, 1985).

33 See Scott Lash, *Sociology of Postmodernism* (London and New York: Routledge, 1990), pp. 55f.

34 Michel Foucault, *The Order of Things: An Archeology of the Human Sciences* (New York: Vintage Books, 1973).

35 This is discussed in David Lyon, 'Bentham's Panopticon: From Moral Architecture to Electronic Surveillance', *The Queen's Quarterly*, 98:3, 1991; and in 'An Electronic Panopticon: A Sociological Critique of Surveillance Theory', *The Sociological Review*, 41:4, 1993.

36 See Zygmunt Bauman, *Postmodernity and its Discontents* (New York: New York University Press, 1997).

37 Jean Baudrillard, *Forget Foucault* (New York: Semiotext(e), 1987).

38 The best introduction to Baudrillard in his own words is Mark Poster, *Jean Baudrillard: Selected Writings* (Cambridge: Polity Press, and Stanford, CA: Stanford University Press, 1988).

39 Jean Baudrillard, *The Mirror of Production* (St Louis: Telos, 1975), p. 144. First published in French in 1973.

40 See Jean Baudrillard, *For a Critique of the Political Economy of the Sign* (St Louis: Telos, 1981). First published in French in 1972.

41 Alain Touraine, *Critique of Modernity* (Oxford: Blackwell, 1995), p. 144.

42 See Manuel Castells, *The Power of Identity* (Oxford: Blackwell, 1997);

Craig Calhoun (ed.), *Social Theory and the Politics of Identity* (Oxford: Blackwell, 1994).

43 See, for example, Mark Poster, *The Mode of Information* (Cambridge: Polity Press, 1990), Chapter 2.

44 See, for example, Martin Jay, *Forcefields* (London and New York: Routledge, 1993), pp. 90–8; Bauman, *Intimations*, p. 155; and Bryan Turner and Chris Rojek (eds), *Forget Baudrillard* (London and New York: Routledge, 1993).

45 The quotation is from Arthur Kroker, Marielouise Kroker and David Cook (eds), *Panic Encyclopedia* (Montreal: New World Perspectives, 1989), pp. 13, 16. Kroker is probably best known for his *The Postmodern Scene: Excremental Culture and Hyper-Aesthetics* (Montreal: New World Perspectives, 1988).

46 Bryan Turner (ed.), *Theories of Modernity and Postmodernity* (London and Beverly Hills, CA: Sage, 1990), p. 10; and Barry Smart, 'Europe/America: Baudrillard's Fatal Comparison', in Turner and Rojek, *Forget Baudrillard*.

47 Berman, *All that is Solid Melts into Air*, London and New York: Penguin, 1988 (orig. 1982), p. 35.

Chapter 3

1 Barry Smart, 'Modernity, Postmodernity and the Present' in Bryan Turner (ed.), *Theories of Modernity and Postmodernity* (London and Newbury Park, CA: Sage, 1990), p. 17.

2 Peter Berger, *Pyramids of Sacrifice* (New York: Basic Books, 1975).

3 Walt W. Rostow, *The Stages of Economic Growth* (Cambridge: Cambridge University Press, 1960).

4 Daniel Lerner, *The Passing of Traditional Society* (Glencoe, IL: The Free Press, 1958).

5 Krishan Kumar makes this point in *Prophecy and Progress: The Sociology of Industrial and Postindustrial Society* (Harmondsworth: Penguin, 1978), p. 55.

6 Roland Robertson, *Talcott Parsons: Theorist of Modernity* (London and Newbury Park, CA: Sage, 1991).

7 Quoted in Kumar, *Prophecy and Progress*, p. 71.

8 Le Corbusier, *The City of Tomorrow* [1929] (Cambridge, MA: MIT Press, 1971), p. 4.

9 See Christopher Dandeker, *Surveillance, Power and Modernity* (Cambridge: Polity Press, 1990).

10 Richard V. Ericson and Kevin D. Haggerty, *Policing the Risk Society* (Toronto: University of Toronto Press, 1997), p. 97.

11 Norbert Elias, *The Civilizing Process* (Oxford: Blackwell, 1978).

12 Michel Foucault, *Discipline and Punish: The Birth of the Prison* (New

York: Vintage Books, 1979). This is critically discussed by a number authors including Michael Ignatieff, *A Just Measure of Pain* (New York: Pantheon, 1978), and, in relation to electronic technologies, David Lyon, *The Electronic Eye: The Rise of Surveillance Society*, Cambridge: Polity Press, and Minneapolis: University of Minnesota Press, 1994).

13 de Tocqueville quoted in Krishan Kumar (ed.), *Revolution: The Theory and Practice of a European Idea* (London: Weidenfeld and Nicholson, 1971), p. 115.

14 In subsequent work, Giddens does not neglect the factors mentioned here. Globalization is a prominent feature of the newer editions of his textbook, *Introduction to Sociology* (New York and London: W. W. Norton, 1996). Gender is discussed in *The Transformation of Intimacy: Sexuality, Love and Eroticism in Modern Societies* (Cambridge: Polity Press; Stanford: Stanford University Press, 1992). And religion is discussed in his *Modernity and Self-Identity* (Cambridge: Polity Press, 1991). But these three factors, especially religion, remain unintegrated into his overall conceptual scheme for understanding modernity. Stejpan Meštrovíc, *Anthony Giddens: The Last Modernist* (New York: Routledge, 1998).

15 Though it is a less well-known contribution than some of his others, Freud's *Civilization and its Discontents*, with its pessimism about revolutionary socialism, can also count as a negative judgement on modernity. Hence my echo of it in the chapter title.

16 'Modes of production and regimes of regulation' are discussed by David Harvey in *The Postmodern Condition* (Oxford, UK, and Cambridge, MA: Basil Blackwell, 1990), Chapter 5.

17 Peter Berger, *The Homeless Mind* (Harmondsworth: Penguin, 1974).

18 Sociology as legislative and as interpretive reason is discussed by Zygmunt Bauman in *Legislators and Interpreters* (Cambridge: Polity Press, 1987) and in *Intimations of Postmodernity* (London and Boston: Routledge, 1992), Chapter 5.

19 Quoted in Robert Nisbet, *The Sociological Tradition* (London: Heinemann, and New York: Basic Books, 1967), p. 299.

20 Jacques Ellul's classic treatment is in *The Technological Society* (New York: Vintage, 1964).

21 See Zygmunt Bauman, *Modernity and the Holocaust* (Cambridge: Polity Press, 1989); George Ritzer, *The Big Mac Attack: The McDonaldization of Society* (New York: Lexington Books, 1992).

22 Charles Baudelaire, *Selected Writings on Art and Artists* (Harmondsworth: Penguin, 1981).

23 Frederic Engels, *The Condition of the Working Classes in England* [1848] (Oxford: Blackwell, 1951).

24 Quoted in Kumar, *Prophesy and Progress*, p. 64.

Madan Sarup, *Identity, Culture, and the Postmodern World* (Edinburgh: Edinburgh University Press, 1996), p. 10.

26 Bryan Turner, *Orientalism, Postmodernism and Globalism* (London and New York: Routledge, 1994), p. 95.

27 Charles Taylor, *The Malaise of Modernity* (Toronto: Anansi, 1991).

28 John Beniger, *The Control Revolution* (Cambridge, MA: MIT Press, 1986).

29 John Keats, 'Lamia' l. 230.

30 Giddens, *Modernity and Self-Identity*, p. 9.

31 Matthew Arnold, 'Dover Beach', *Poetry and Prose* (London: Hart-Davis, 1958), pp. 144–5.

32 Bruno Latour, *We have Never Been Modern* (New York and London: Harvester-Wheatsheaf, 1993). English translation of *Nous n'avons jamais étés modernes* (Paris: La Découverte, 1991).

33 Alain Touraine, *Critique of Modernity* (Oxford, and Cambridge, MA: Blackwell, 1995), p. 366. English translation of *Une critique de la modernité* (Paris: Fayard, 1992).

34 Ulrich Beck, *Risk Society: Towards a New Modernity* (London: Sage, 1992).

35 Ibid., p. 176.

36 Ulrich Beck, Anthony Giddens and Scott Lash, *Reflexive Modernization: Politics, Tradition, and Aesthetics in the Modern Social Order* (Cambridge: Polity Press, 1994).

Chapter 4

1 Daniel Bell, *The Coming of Postindustrial Society* (New York: Basic Books, 1973), p. 137.

2 Daniel Bell, *The Cultural Contradictions of Capitalism* (New York: Basic Books, 1976). This is discussed helpfully by Bryan Turner, 'From Post-industrial Society to Postmodern Politics' in John Gibbin (ed.), *Contemporary Political Culture* (London and Newbury Park, CA: Sage, 1989).

3 Daniel Bell, 'The Social Framework of the Information Society' in Tom Forester (ed.), *The Information Technology Revolution* (Oxford: Blackwell, and Cambridge, MA: MIT Press, 1980).

4 This shift is discussed in David Lyon 'From Postindustrialism to Information Society: A New Social Transformation?', *Sociology*, 20:4, 1986, pp. 577–88; and David Lyon, *The Information Society: Issues and Illusions* (Cambridge: Polity Press, 1988, and New York: Basil Blackwell, 1989), also as *La Società dell'Informazione* (Bologna: il Mulino, 1991).

5 See, for example, David Lyon, 'The Information Society Concept in Public Policy' in Frank Gregory and Raymond Plant (eds), *Information Technology: The Public Issues* (Manchester: Manchester University Press, 1988).

Notes

6 Arthur Cordell, *Planning Now for the Information Society*, Report ~
33 (Ottawa: Science Council of Canada, 1982); Arthur Cordell, *Th*
Uneasy Eighties: The Transition to an Information Society, Study no. 5~
(Ottawa: Science Council of Canada, 1985).

7 The information economy was discussed by authors such as Marc Porat,
The Information Economy: Definition and Measurement (Washington
DC: US Office of Commerce, 1977), but also in Bell's work and the
well-known report by Simon Nora and Alain Minc, *L'Informatisation*
de la société (Paris: La Documentation Française, 1980).

8 Lucie Deschênes, *Towards an Information Society*, Canadian Workplace Automation Research Centre (Ottawa: Communication Canada,
1992), p. 1.

9 Ibid., p. 47.

10 John Goyder, *Essentials of Canadian Society* (Toronto: McLelland and
Stewart, 1990), Chapter 9.

11 Industry Profile. Canada's Information Technology Sector, Statistics
Canada, Catalogue 15-516-MPE, May 1996, p. 1.

12 'Measuring the Global Infrastructure for a Global Information Society:
Concepts and Indicators', a paper submitted to the OECD by Canada,
September 1996, p. 261.

13 *Resource Book for Science and Technology Consultations*, vol. 1
(Ottawa: Secretariat for Science and Technology Review, Industry
Canada, June 1994), p. 28.

14 Krishan Kumar, *Prophecy and Progress: The Sociology of Industrial*
and Postindustrial Society (Harmondsworth: Penguin, 1978); Ian Miles
and Jay Gershuny, *The New Service Economy* (London: Frances Pinter,
1983).

15 See, for example, John Kenneth Galbraith, *The New Industrial State*
(Harmondsworth: Penguin, 1969); and Lyon, *Information Society*, pp.
26–30.

16 On this, see also William Leiss, *Under Technology's Thumb* (Montreal
and Kingston: McGill-Queen's University Press, 1990), pp. 131f.

17 Mark Hepworth seems sanguine about this in his *The Geography of the*
Information Economy (London: Belhaven Press, 1989).

18 See Rowland Lorimer and Jean McNulty, *Mass Communication in*
Canada, 2nd edn (Toronto: McClelland and Stewart, 1991), p. 274.

19 See Doreen Massey, Paul Quintas and David Wield, *High Tech Fan-*
tasies: Technology Parks in Science, Society and Space (London: Routledge, 1992), p. 9 and Chapter 5.

20 *Maclean's*, 15 March 1993, pp. 30–1. See also 'The Silicon Coast', *Globe*
and Mail Report on Business, 30 April 1993.

21 Zygmunt Bauman, *Globalization: The Human Consequences* (Cambridge: Polity Press; New York: Columbia University Press, 1998), p. 3.

22 See David Lyon, 'The Electronic Panopticon: A Sociological Critique

of Surveillance Theory', *Sociological Review*, 41:3, 1993; and David Lyon, *The Electronic Eye: The Rise of Surveillance Society* (Cambridge: Polity Press, and Minneapolis: University of Minnesota Press, 1994).

23 See, for example, Oscar Gandy, *The Panoptic Sort: A Political Economy of Personal Information* (Boulder, CO: Westview Press, 1993).

24 Arthur Cordell, 'The Rise of the Infobot', *Policy Options*, May 1991, p. 34.

25 See Benjamin Woolley, *Virtual Worlds* (Oxford, UK, and Cambridge, MA: Blackwell, 1992) for discussion of some other aspects of virtuality.

26 Arthur Cordell, 'The Perils of an Information Age', *Policy Options*, April 1991, p. 19.

27 Tom Forester, 'Megatrends or Megamistakes: Whatever Happened to the Information Society?', *Computers and Society*, 22:1–4, 1992, p. 2.

28 For instance Peter Hall and Paschal Preston, *The Carrier Wave: New Information Technology and the Geography of Innovation 1846–2003* (London, and Winchester, MA: Unwin-Hyman, 1988).

29 On the issue of risks, see Ulrich Beck, *The Risk Society* (Beverly Hills, CA, and London: Sage, 1992).

30 Jean-François Lyotard, *The Postmodern Condition: A Report on Knowledge* (Minneapolis: University of Minnesota Press, and Manchester: University of Manchester Press, 1984) pp. 7, 3, 7.

31 Ibid., p. 46; see also Margaret Rose, *The Postmodern and the Postindustrial: A Critical Analysis* (Cambridge and New York: Cambridge University Press, 1991), p. 31.

32 Lyotard, *Postmodern Condition*, p. 48.

33 Kevin Robins and Frank Webster, *The Technical Fix: Education, Computers and Industry* (London: Macmillan, 1989), p. 140.

34 Lyotard, *Postmodern Condition*, p. 4.

35 Ibid.

36 Ibid.

37 Those discussing post-Fordism include on the one hand sociologists such as Scott Lash and John Urry in *The End of Organized Capitalism* (Cambridge: Polity, 1987), and David Harvey in *The Condition of Postmodernity* (New York: Blackwell, 1990). As a Marxist, the latter is sure that capitalism is still more organized than the former allow.

38 Barry Smart, *Modern Conditions, Postmodern Controversies* (London and New York: Routledge, 1992), p. 141.

39 Others who connect items from the debate over postindustrialism with the question of postmodernity include David Harvey, in *The Condition of Postmodernity*; and Fredric Jameson, *Postmodernism or the Cultural Logic of Late Capitalism* (London: Verso, 1991).

40 Mark Poster, *The Mode of Information: Poststructuralism and Social Context* (Cambridge: Polity Press, 1990).

41 Ibid., p. 14.

42 Ibid., p. 148.

43 This is discussed further in Lyon 'An Electronic Panopticon'.

44 See William Bogard, *The Simulation of Surveillance* (New York: Cambridge University Press, 1996).

45 Poster, *The Mode of Information*, p. 154.

46 David Lyon, 'Cyberspace Sociality: Controversies over Computer-mediated Communication' in Brian Loader (ed.), *The Governance of Cyberspace* (London and New York: Routledge, 1997).

47 The end of the social is further discussed in Smart, *Postmodernity* (London and New York: Routledge, 1993), pp. 51–6.

48 Anthony Giddens, *Modernity and Self Identity* (Cambridge: Polity Press, 1991), p. 26.

49 Decoding TV is discussed in terms of social-class difference, for instance in David Morley, 'Cultural Transformations' in Howard Davis and Paul Walton (eds), *Language, Image, Media* (New York: St Martin's Press, and Oxford: Blackwell, 1983).

50 Mike Featherstone, *Undoing Culture: Globalization, Postmodernism, and Identity* (London: Sage, 1995), p. 117.

51 Gianni Vattimo, *The Transparent Society* (Cambridge: Polity Press, 1992), p. 1.

52 Ibid., p. 5.

53 Ibid., p. 7.

54 Roland Robertson, 'After Nostalgia?' in Bryan Turner (ed.), *Theories of Modernity and Postmodernity* (London and Newbury Park, CA: Sage, 1990), p. 57. Not having any fixed sense of 'humanity' also raises difficulties for Forester's proposed 'humanization of technology', mentioned earlier; an issue for (post)modern ethics to tackle.

55 Immanuel Wallerstein, *The Modern World System*, 3 vols (New York: Academic Press, 1974, 1980, 1989).

56 Mike Featherstone and Scott Lash, 'An Introduction' in Mike Featherstone, Scott Lash and Roland Robertson (eds), *Global Modernities* (London: Sage, 1995), p. 3.

57 I refer to the work of Paul Freston, 'Evangelicalism and Globalization' in Mark Hutchinson and Ogbu Kalu (eds), *A Global Faith* (Sydney: CSAC, 1998).

58 Krishan Kumar, *From Postindustrial to Postmodern Society* (Oxford, UK, and Cambridge, MA: Blackwell, 1995), p. 194.

59 Martin Albrow, *The Global Age* (Cambridge: Polity Press, 1996).

60 Bruno Latour, *We Never were Modern* (New York and London: Harvester-Wheatsheaf, 1993). English translation of *Nous n'avons jamais étés modernes* (Paris: La Découverte, 1991).

61 See Timothy Luke and Steven White, 'Critical Theory, the Informational Revolution and an Ecological Path to Postmodernity' in John Forrester (ed.), *Critical Theory and Public Life* (Cambridge, MA: MIT Press, 1985).

Jean Baudrillard, *La Guerre du Golfe n'as pas eu lieu* (Paris: Galilée, 1991). See comments in Mike Gane, *Baudrillard Live* (London: Routledge, 1993); and an alternative view in Doug Kellner, *The Media War in the Gulf* (Boulder, CO: Westview, 1992).

63 See Featherstone, *Undoing Culture*, pp. 88–9.
64 Vattimo, among others, makes reference to Babel with reference to the 'communicative society'. In the biblical story, efforts to reach heaven by technological mastery were thwarted by a divine confusion of language. So the supposed 'gateway to God' (Babel) became 'balel' (= confusion, Hebrew). A limited emancipation *is* present here, in that the conditions for total domination are eliminated. Vattimo, however, foresees no 'pentecostal reversal' of this.
65 This is discussed in Vattimo, *The Transparent Society*, pp. 105–17. See also Martin Jay, *Forcefields* (London: Routledge, 1993), pp. 38–48.
66 The point is well made by Leiss, *Under Technology's Thumb*, p. 148.

Chapter 5

1 Jean Baudrillard, *America* (London and New York: Verso, 1988), pp. 123–4.
2 Stjepan Meštrović, *The Barbarian Temperament* (London and New York: Routledge, 1993), especially Chapter 1. Veblen's critique starts by denying that 'barbarism' can ever be contained by 'civilization'. Human beings remain as *homo duplex*, capable of both good and evil. So the modern mistake is to obscure barbarism in modern culture, and the postmodern, to deny culture, good or bad (p. 22).
3 Iain Chambers, quoted in David Harvey, *The Condition of Postmodernity* (New York: Blackwell, 1990), p. 61.
4 Mike Featherstone, *Consumer Culture and Postmodernism* (London and Beverly Hills, CA: Sage, 1991), p. 48.
5 Harvey, *The Condition of Postmodernity*, p. 61.
6 Baudrillard's work is excerpted usefully, and helpfully introduced, in Mark Poster's edited collection, *Jean Baudrillard: Selected Writings* (Cambridge: Polity Press, 1988).
7 Brian McHale, *Postmodernist Fiction* (London and New York: Methuen, 1987).
8 City culture is discussed in Chapter 7 of Featherstone, *Consumer Culture and Postmodernism*.
9 Harvey, *The Condition of Postmodernity*, p. 39.
10 See John Urry, *The Tourist Gaze: Leisure and Travel in Contemporary Society* (London and Newbury Park, CA: Sage, 1990).
11 Edward Soja, *Postmodern Geographies* (London and New York: Verso, 1989), p. 221.

12 Harvey takes Jonathan Raban's *Soft City* (London: Fontana, 1974) to
be a crucial turning point in understanding contemporary urbanism.

13 Mike Davis, *City of Quartz* (London: Verso, 1988).

14 Anthony Giddens, *Modernity and Self-Identity* (Cambridge: Polity
Press, 1991), p. 198.

15 Philip Sampson, 'Postmodernity' in Lars Johannson (ed.), *Modernity*, 1st
edn, forthcoming from 1993 Lausanne Consultation, Uppsala, Sweden.

16 W. B. Yeats, 'The Second Coming', from *Selected Poetry*, ed. Norman
Jeffares (London: Macmillan, 1965), p. 99.

17 Peter Berger, *The Heretical Imperative* (New York: Doubleday, 1980).

18 Barry Smart, *Postmodernity* (London and New York: Routledge, 1993),
p. 111.

19 Reginald Bibby, *Fragmented Gods: The Poverty and Potential of
Religion in Canada* (Toronto: Irwin, 1987).

20 See David Lyon, 'A Bit of a Circus: Postmodernity and New Age',
Religion, 23:2, 1993.

21 *The Persistence of Faith* was the theme of Jonathan Sacks' BBC Reith
Lectures (London: Weidenfeld and Nicholson, 1991).

22 Smart, *Postmodernity*, p. 120, makes a similar point.

23 Roy Clements, 'Can Tolerance Become the Enemy of Christian
Freedom?', *Cambridge Papers*, 1:1, 1992.

24 Jean-François Lyotard, *The Postmodern Condition: A Report on Knowledge* (Minneapolis: University of Minnesota Press, and Manchester:
University of Manchester Press, 1984), p. 40.

25 *Science Wars* was the title given to a special issue of *Social Text*, 14: 1–2,
1996.

26 Thomas Kuhn, *The Structure of Scientific Revolutions* (Minneapolis:
University of Minnesota Press, 1960).

27 This account follows that of Hilary Lawson in his coedited book (with
Lisa Appignanesi) *Dismantling Truth: Reality in the Postmodern World*
(London: Weidenfeld and Nicholson, 1989).

28 Richard Rorty, *Philosophy and the Mirror of Nature* (Princeton: Princeton University Press, 1979).

29 Ibid., p. 179.

30 *New York Review of Books*, 8 August 1996, pp. 11–15.

31 Bruno Latour, *Science in Action* (Milton Keynes: Open University
Press, 1987), p. 79.

32 See, for example, Evelyn Fox-Keller, *Reflections on Gender and Science*
(New Haven: Yale University Press, 1985).

33 See, for example, Nancy Fraser and Linda Nicholson, 'Social Criticism
without Philosophy: An Encounter between Postmodernism and
Feminism' in Linda Nicholson (ed.), *Feminism/Postmodernism*
(London and New York: Routledge, 1990).

34 Susan Hekman, *Gender and Knowledge: Elements of a Postmodern Feminism* (Cambridge: Polity Press, 1990).

35 For example, Angela MacRobbie in Lisa Appignanesi (ed.), *Postmodernism: ICA Documents* (London: Free Association Books, 1989).

36 See, for example, Helen Carr reviewing postmodern books in *Red Letters: A Review of Cultural Politics*, no. 25, Winter 1990, p. 6.

37 Mike Featherstone, 'The Body in Consumer Culture' in Mike Featherstone, Mike Hepworth, and Bryan Turner (eds), *The Body: Social Process and Cultural Theory* (London: Sage, 1991), p. 178.

38 Philip Sampson, 'Die Repräsentation des Körpers', ('The Representation of the Body'), *Kunstforum International*, Bd 132, pp. 94–111.

39 Kevin Robins, *Into the Image: Culture and Politics in the Field of Vision* (London and New York: Routledge, 1996), p. 117.

40 See, for example, the journal *Personal Computing* which deals with wearable, portable and implantable electronic machinery.

41 Kevin Warwick's implant was reported in *The Daily Telegraph*, 26 August 1998, p. 3.

42 Donna Haraway, *Simians, Cyborgs, and Women* (London and New York: Routledge, 1991), p. 208.

43 Ibid., p. 212.

44 This is discussed by Anthony Giddens in *The Transformation of Intimacy: Sexuality, Love and Eroticism in Modern Societies* (Cambridge: Polity Press, and Stanford: Stanford University Press, 1992), pp. 28–34.

45 Judith Butler, *Bodies that Matter* (New York and London: Routledge, 1993).

46 Terry Lovell, 'Feminist Social Theory' in Bryan Turner (ed.), *The Blackwell Companion to Social Theory* (Oxford: Blackwell, 1996), p. 334.

47 Manuel Castells, *The Power of Identity* (Oxford: Blackwell, 1997), p. 239.

48 Philip Mellor and Chris Shilling, *Re-forming the Body: Religion, Community and Modernity* (London: Sage, 1997).

49 On this, see Ralf Schroeder, *Possible Worlds: The Social Dynamic of Virtual Reality Technology* (Boulder, CO: Westview, 1996).

50 Mellor and Shilling, *Re-forming the Body*, p. 30.

51 Lovell, 'Feminist Social Theory', p. 337.

52 Fredric Jameson, *Postmodernism or the Cultural Logic of Late Capitalism* (Durham, NC: Duke University Press, 1991).

53 Harvey, *The Condition of Postmodernity*, p. 345.

54 Zygmunt Bauman, *Intimations of Postmodernity* (New York and London: Routledge, 1992).

55 Ibid., p. 49.

56 Pierre Bourdieu, *Distinction: A Social Critique of the Judgement of Taste* (London and New York: Routledge, 1984).

57 Bauman, *Intimations*, p. 155.

58 Ibid., p. 224.
59 See, for example, Douglas Kellner, *Critical Theory, Marxism and Modernity* (Cambridge: Polity Press, 1989), p. 161; and also Anthony Giddens, 'Dare to Care, Conserve and Repair', *New Statesman and Society*, 29 October 1993, pp. 18–20.
60 *The Limits to Satisfaction* is the title of William Leiss's important book (Montreal and Kingston: McGill-Queen's University Press, 1988). In it he challenges Marcuse, arguing that consumption should be central to a critical social theory, because there is cause for concern when 'commodity exchange [becomes] the *exclusive* mode for the satisfaction of needs'. My views on the matter are also influenced by John V. Taylor, *Enough is Enough* (London: SCM, 1975).
61 David Ley and Caroline Mills, 'Can There Be a Postmodernism of Resistance?' in Paul Knox (ed.), *The Restless Urban Landscape* (New York: Prentice-Hall, 1992).
62 See Bryan Turner, *Citizenship* (Milton Keynes: Open University Press, and Minneapolis: University of Minnesota Press, 1991); Ernesto Laclau and Chantal Mouffe, *Dimensions of Radical Democracy: Pluralism, Citizenship, Community* (London: Verso, 1990).
63 Philip Wexler, 'Citizenship in the semiotic society' in Bryan Turner (ed.), *Theories of Modernity and Postmodernity* (London and Newbury Park, CA: Sage, 1990); David Lyon, *The Electronic Eye: The Rise of Surveillance Society* (Cambridge: Polity Press, and Minneapolis: University of Minnesota Press, 1994).
64 Oscar Gandy, *The Panoptic Sort: A Political Economy of Personal Information* (Boulder, CO: Westview Press, 1993).
65 Featherstone, *Consumer Culture and Postmodernism* (London: Sage, 1991), p. 143.
66 Here I am thinking of Bauman, Meštrović and Turner, referred to earlier.
67 Scott Lash, 'Postmodern Ethics: The Missing Ground', *Theory, Culture, and Society*, 13:2, 1996, pp. 91–104.
68 See the introduction to Zygmunt Bauman, *Postmodern Ethics* (Oxford, UK, and Cambridge, MA: Blackwell, 1993).
69 Ibid., p. 13.
70 Colin Campbell, *The Romantic Ethic and the Spirit of Modern Consumerism* (Oxford and New York: Basil Blackwell Inc., 1987). See also Rosalind Williams, *Dreamworlds* (Berkeley and Los Angeles: University of California Press, 1982).

Chapter 6

1 Timothy Findley, *Not Wanted on the Voyage* (Toronto: Viking, 1984).
2 Wolfgang Welsch, *Unsere Moderne Postmoderne* (Berlin: Akademie, 1993).

3 See Roland Robertson, 'The Sociological Significance of Culture: Some General Considerations', _Theory, Culture and Society_, 5:1, 1988, pp. 3–23.
4 See Bryan Turner, 'Periodization and Politics in the Postmodern' in Bryan Turner (ed.), _Theories of Modernity and Postmodernity_ (London and Beverly Hills, CA: Sage, 1990), pp. 8–9.
5 See Stejpan Meštrović, _The Coming Fin de Siècle_ (London and New York: Routledge, 1992). His _The Barbarian Temperament_ (London and New York: Routledge, 1993) examines the 'Christian' themes in Durkheim, Freud and others.
6 David Lyon, 'A Bit of a Circus: Notes on Postmodernity and New Age', _Religion_, 23:2, 1993.
7 See, for example, Kieran Flanagan and Peter Jupp (eds), _Postmodernity, Sociology, and Religion_ (New York: St Martin's Press, 1996); Philippa Berry and Andrew Wernick (eds), _Shadow of Spirit: Postmodernism and Religion_ (New York: Routledge, 1992).
8 Barry Smart, _Modern Conditions, Postmodern Controversies_ (London and New York: Routledge, 1992), p. 5.
9 Susan Sontag, _Illness as Metaphor_ (Harmondsworth: Penguin, 1991), p. 175.
10 Martin Jay, 'The Apocalyptic Imagination and the Inability to Mourn' in _Forcefields_ (London and New York: Routledge, 1992), pp. 84–98.
11 The theme of apocalypse could be said to be present in, for example, Lyotard, who speaks of a 'sorrow in the zeitgeist', and Foucault, with his talk of the 'end' of modern scientific world-views. Certainly French popular media dubbed him a 'millenarian' when these views first appeared. Doubtless he would have denied it.
12 See Ulrich Beck, _The Risk Society_ (London and Newbury Park, CA: Sage, 1992).
13 David Noble, _The Religion of Technology_ (New York: Knopf, 1997); Donna Haraway, _Modest_Witness@Second_Millennium.FemaleMan_Meets_Oncomouse_ (New York and London: Routledge, 1997).
14 Haraway, _Modest_Witness@Second_Millennium_, p. 10.
15 Robertson, 'Sociological Significance', p. 19.
16 Mike Featherstone, _Consumer Culture and Postmodernism_ (London and Beverly Hills, CA: Sage, 1991), p. 27.
17 Douglas Kellner, 'Boundaries and Borderlines: Reflections on Jean Baudrillard and Critical Theory', _Current Perspectives in Social Theory_, 9, 1989, pp. 5–22.
18 Zygmunt Bauman, _Legislators and Interpreters_ (Cambridge: Polity Press, 1988).
19 Gianni Vattimo, _The End of Modernity_ (Cambridge: Polity Press, and Baltimore: The Johns Hopkins University Press, 1988), p. 177.
20 Turner, 'Periodization and Politics', p. 12.

21 David Harvey, *The Condition of Postmodernity* (Oxford, UK, and Cambridge, MA: Blackwell, 1990), p. 44.
22 Eco, cited in Krishan Kumar, *From Post-Industrial to Post-Modern Society* (Oxford and New York: Basil Blackwell, 1995), p. 124.
23 Venturi, quoted Harvey, *The Condition of Postmodernity*, p. 60.
24 Foucault in Paul Rabinow (ed.), *The Foucault Reader* (Harmondsworth: Penguin, 1984).
25 Gianni Vattimo, *The Transparent Society* (Cambridge: Polity Press, 1992).
26 Ibid., p. 7.
27 Ibid., p. 11.
28 Richard Rorty, *Objectivity, Relativism, and Truth* (Cambridge: Cambridge University Press, 1991), p. 1.
29 Douglas Kellner, 'Postmodernism as Social Theory: Some Challenges and Problems', *Theory, Culture and Society*, 5: 2–3, 1988.
30 Edward Said, *Orientalism* (New York: Pantheon, 1979).
31 Madan Sarup, *Identity, Culture and the Postmodern World* (Edinburgh: Edinburgh University Press, 1996), p. xvi.
32 Satya Mohanty, 'Colonial Legacies, Multicultural Futures: Relativism, Objectivity, and the Challenge of Otherness', *Publications of the Modern Language Association of America*, 110:1, 1995, p. 113.
33 Arthur Kroker, *The Possessed Individual: Technology and the French Postmodern* (Montreal: New World Perspectives, 1992), p. 165.
34 See, for example, Martin Jay, 'Is there a Poststructuralist Ethics?' in *Forcefields* (London and New York: Routledge, 1993).
35 I have in mind Douglas Kellner, *Critical Theory, Marxism and Modernity* (Cambridge: Polity Press, 1988); Mark Poster, *Critical Theory and Poststructuralism* (Ithaca, NY: Cornell University Press, 1989); and, in parallel with this, feminist work such as Linda Nicholson (ed.), *Feminism/Postmodernism* (New York and London: Routledge, 1990).
36 Ernest Gellner, *Postmodernism, Reason and Religion* (London and New York: Routledge, 1992).
37 Richard Bernstein, *Habermas and Modernity* (Cambridge: Polity Press, and Cambridge, MA: MIT Press, 1985), p. 31.
38 Jürgen Habermas in ibid., p. 94.
39 Jürgen Habermas, *The Philosophical Discourses of Modernity* (Cambridge, MA: MIT Press, 1987), pp. 4–5.
40 Anthony Giddens, *The Consequences of Modernity* (Cambridge: Polity Press, 1990).
41 David Lyon, 'Bentham's Panopticon: From Moral Architecture to Electronic Surveillance', *Queen's Quarterly*, 98:3, 1991; Martin Jay, 'In the Empire of the Gaze: Foucault and the Denigration of Vision in Twentieth Century French Thought', in David Couzens Hoy, *Foucault: A Critical Reader* (London and New York: Blackwell, 1986).

42 Frederic Jameson, *Postmodernism, or, The Cultural Logic of Late Capitalism* (Durham, NC: Duke University Press, 1991).

43 Nicholson, *Feminism/Postmodernism*, p. 2.

44 Charles Taylor, *The Malaise of Modernity* (Toronto: Anansi/CBC, 1991).

45 Ann Game, *Undoing the Social: Towards a Deconstructive Sociology* (Buckingham: Open University Press, and Toronto: UTP, 1991), p. 18.

46 Keith Tester, *The Life and Times of Postmodernity* (London and New York: Routledge, 1993), p. 152.

47 Featherstone, *Consumer Culture and Postmodernism*, p. ix.

48 Zygmunt Bauman, *Intimations of Postmodernity* (London: Routledge, 1992).

49 Ibid., p. 111.

50 Alasdair MacIntyre, *After Virtue* (London: Duckworth, 1981), p. 111.

51 Bernstein, *Habermas and Modernity*, pp. 118f.

52 Charles Taylor, *The Malaise of Modernity* (Toronto: Anansi, 1991).

53 Jean-François Lyotard and Jean-Loup Thébaud, *Just Gaming* (Minneapolis: University of Minnesota Press, 1985), p. 14.

54 Roy Boyne, *Foucault and Derrida: The Other Side of Reason* (London and Winchester, MA: Unwin-Hyman, 1990), p. 150.

55 See Jay, *Forcefields*, pp. 40f.

56 George Grant, *Technology and Empire* (Toronto: Anansi, 1969). See also Peter Self, 'George Grant: Unique Canadian Philosopher', *Queen's Quarterly*, 98:1, 1991, pp. 25–39.

57 David Lyon, 'Beyond Secular Reason: Milbank on Augustine and Postmodernity', *Crux*, September 1992.

58 See Philip Abrams, *Historical Sociology* (Shepton Mallet, Somerset: Open Books, 1982), where he discusses the 'problematic' as a rudimentary organization of a field of study that yields clues as to what is important and what peripheral.

59 There is no doubt that the term 'Judeo-Christian' is a controversial means of connecting one religious tradition with another. But whether or not it is a false appropriation is a religious question. The fact that it has sometimes involved uncordial and conflictual relations in no way excludes the possibility, intended here, of mutual recognition and respect.

60 Neighbour-love connects closely with compassion (and thus with Bauman's concern for sufferers) and is discussed in relation to Schopenhauer by Meštrović, *The Coming Fin de Siècle*, pp. 62f. Responsibility also has Judeo-Christian roots, as I understand it, and is discussed, *inter alia*, by Hans Jonas in *The Imperative of Responsibility* (Chicago: University of Chicago Press, 1984), in relation to a Christian perspective on technology in Stephen Monsma (ed.), *Responsible Technology* (Grand Rapids, MI: Eerdmans, 1986), and to postmodernity in Keith Tester, *The Life and Times of Postmodernity* (London and New York: Routledge, 1993), Chapter 5.

Index